VOICE & VISION

Use Your Voice to Bring Your Vision to Life

Phoebe Fazio

Cover design by 100 Covers

Printed in the United States of America
ISBN: 979-8-9968629-0-0

https://phoebefazio.com

Contents

INTRODUCTION

My Journey

After decades of teaching music in public schools, I hit one of the lowest points of my career. A parent of one of my students—someone I considered a close friend—betrayed me, telling other parents and the administration that I verbally abused her daughter and other students. The accusation shook me to the core. Even after decades of high praise for my teaching, I suddenly doubted myself and everything I was passionate about. Unsure of how to go on, I found myself in a therapist's office. Again.

I'd already been in and out of therapy to help with my severe stage fright as a music major in college, but this time was different. Although I didn't know the term at that time, I was in a dark night of my soul. My suffering was so intense, I was open to anything that might alleviate it, so when the therapist offered to try something different—something that would work faster than talk therapy—I readily accepted.

What followed was unlike anything I'd ever experienced. At the therapist's guidance, I lay down on a massage table while she waved her hands over me. After a few minutes, I closed my eyes and heard what I later learned were crystal bowls as well as unusual sounds that the therapist made with her voice. I had no idea what she was doing, but afterward I felt better. Much better.

I continued with these treatments, and after a few sessions, I found myself spontaneously making sounds with my voice while hearing and feeling the sounds of the crystal bowls. I felt like my voice was playing in the sound waves from the bowls the way dolphins play in the waves of the ocean.

Before these sessions, I was not on a spiritual path (at least not consciously). I didn't know anything about energy healing, chakras, or voice and vision (in a spiritual sense). However, this therapist guided me to discover that I was a very spiritual person, and she helped me discover my spiritual gifts. She told me we'd been working with energy and sound healing and that the sounds I made with my voice were called *toning*. She also taught me about the seven chakras (the body's energy centers, traditionally positioned along the spine) and the corresponding vowel sounds for each one.

I had no idea where any of this was going, but I continued on my own, making the sounds from our sessions and toning my chakras. However, as powerful as this practice was when I did it in private, I wanted to share about it with others. So I joined a local spiritual center and an online community where I connected with like-minded people and talked about my experiences. As I did, several members intuitively told me that I was going to help people with my voice—but they didn't know what that looked like, and neither did I.

So, in my newly started meditation practice and prayers, I asked, "How can I help people?" The answer I kept getting was, "Just do it." Just do *what?* I wondered. For many months, I didn't receive any specific guidance. Nonetheless, I kept showing up—meditating, praying, and continuing the toning. Then, one afternoon while driving home from Mt. Shasta and listening to a CD called *Vocal Toning the Chakras*, I suddenly understood what I could do: a daily practice of toning my chakras—which I began immediately.

After a few years of daily chakra-toning, I was invited to teach something to a few individuals online. I didn't know what I wanted to teach, so I asked three friends if they were willing to go along for the ride as I figured it out intuitively. They agreed, and I started by teaching them how to tone their chakras.

After we did this, we sat in silence and I was guided to ask them, "What is your highest vision?" This visioning was not like setting goals or making a vision board. This was sitting in the stillness and asking our highest self (God, Spirit, Divine, etc.) what their vision for us looked like. After my friends asked, they sat and received whatever came. Sometimes the vision showed up as a mental picture, but it could also present itself as a feeling, an idea, or a knowing. However it showed up for them, I coached them to accept it and welcome it into their hearts.

As I continued guiding my friends in this practice, they began to not just see the vision; they *entered* it. They felt themselves inside the vision, where they could see it, hear it, taste it, touch it. They could even rise above that scene to see the bigger picture, how they got there, and what was next—almost like lucid dreaming, where the dreamer is conscious that they are dreaming and can make active decisions during the dream. This type of visioning allowed them to look into their vision and ask questions for clarity.

All three of my willing participants connected with their highest vision in different ways, but each had a profound experience. Two of them had visions related to where they were headed with their healing business. The third person's vision was more spiritual, yet it also impacted the direction of her spiritual business.

After those initial teaching sessions, I continued to support my first three students as well as many others through one-on-one and group coaching programs. Using voice and vision, I've guided clients to discover their vision and their next steps, including personal development, spiritual growth, and practical measures to clarify and market their offerings. Later, I offered my Proven 3-Step Process to live your vision (which is available for free on my website for all who wish to try it: phoebefazio.com/book-extras). And on a personal level, I truly discovered my own voice.

Through the years, I've discovered that the voice is a powerful vehicle to transport you into your vision, allowing you to really live it and express yourself in the real world as your highest version of yourself. Your own voice, which is always with you, becomes a tool for discovering, tapping into, and sharing your highest vision.

Looking back, it's amazing to think that this all arose from my dark night of the soul. What began as a low point ultimately led me and others to new heights.

Your Journey

What about you?

- Do you know what your highest vision is?
- Is this something you're looking for?
- Do you feel like something is holding you back from sharing your vision?
- Is it your voice that's holding you back from sharing your message on stage, in videos, or audio recordings?

This book could be the thing that helps you use your voice to bring your vision to life, whether it's for a business or to bring a greater sense of purpose to your life.

I've helped many others discover, share, and live their visions, and I know that this process can work for you too.

What to Expect from This Book

Throughout this book, I'll walk you through every step of the process, holding your hand through the places that feel scary or treacherous to help you discover your highest vision and bring it to life in your own way.

I'll share stories of how this process has affected my life and then bring it back to you, inviting you to dive in deeper with your own practice and to play with your voice, in your journal, and in business or other areas of life.

In my own journey, I started with the seven chakras then moved into vision, so I'll guide you to do that as well. Later, we'll go deeper with the Visioning Process and also explore the twelve-chakra system that came into my life when I was ready. Throughout this journey, remember that I didn't know anything about any of this at first, so I'll gently guide you as you discover and explore all this at a comfortable pace.

Whether you go through the book page by page, doing all the playful activities, or use your intuition to guide you to the parts that call to you, you'll find exactly what you're looking for and needing.

The most important thing is to get started. So, turn the page and take the first step. Then see where you're guided next. And remember, I'll be right here with you every step of the way.

PART ONE: Invitation to Test the Waters

I. Voice:
Exploring Simple Sounds of the Seven Chakras

1. It All Starts with the Breath

Making sound with our own voice can bring up some concerns, so let's start by just taking a few deep breaths.

Close your eyes and really tune in to your breathing for three or four breaths. No place to get to, just tuning in to the way you're breathing right now.

- What do you notice about your breathing?
- Where in your body do you feel the expansion of the inhale?
- Can you follow that expansion?
- Can you allow more places to open?
- As you notice your breaths, do you notice something shifting in you?
- Do you feel more relaxed? Or is it causing more tension?

If you notice tension, let that be okay. Let yourself feel that. In that acceptance, sometimes we can feel a gentle letting go. No worries if you don't. Stay with the sensations you are having. If this exercise is uncomfortable or triggering, don't stay with those sensations. Perhaps get up and go for a walk. Reach out to a trusted friend to talk about what you felt. And maybe try again with a friend nearby or some other comforts.

I've noticed that, over time, the sounds I make have deepened my breathing—most likely a result of the attention

I'm giving to my breath. The more I've practiced, the more expansive my lung capacity has become. This allows me to sustain a sound longer with more ease. So, if you're concerned with how much lung capacity you have, I invite you to allow the process to work for you in time.

I feel that sustaining sounds is more about the breath than about the sound or any technique. So, as we start making sound, if you notice tension—or if you get distracted or lost in thought—come back to your breath. It's all okay; you're not doing it wrong. There is no right or wrong in how you make the sounds. No one is judging you. And if you do notice an inner judge, I invite you to ask it to go do something else. You don't need that while you do this voice practice. (We'll explore this idea more in the "How Do You Befriend Your Inner Critic?" chapter, but you can read that now if you're called to.)

While you're making the sounds, allow yourself to inhale and exhale as often as you feel the need. There's no rush. In fact, I find that the slower I go, the more fascinating it is. I can feel more, I can go deeper, and I enjoy the sounds even more. Even when you think you're going slow, see if you can go even slower.

The sounds are usually made on the exhale, so your best sounds will come when you have a full, complete inhale to start. And if you find it challenging to sustain a sound, take note of that. Inhale again in an easy, gentle, relaxed way and make the sound again. And again. It may shift after a few times.

If you sustain a sound and feel the need to have a breath in between repeating the sound, then I give you permission to take a breath in between. Keep it easy and relaxed.

When I do my Voice Expression practice while I'm walking, I find that I need an extra breath between tones. If I'm completely relaxed, whether seated or lying down, I feel like I can sustain a sound for a very long time.

I even notice that each chakra can feel different, and therefore the sound comes out differently—a louder or softer volume, a different quality, more or less effort. That may happen for you as well. Whatever you experience is perfectly okay. It's all helpful information.

Let's Play!

Have you done any kind of breathwork before? If you have, then you may have done some of these. If you haven't, no worries. Here are a few exercises you can do to allow your breath to feel more at ease and more powerful:

Box Breathing

Breathe in for a count of four.

Hold for a count of four.

Breathe out for a count of four.

Hold for a count of four.

Star Breathing

Using your pointer finger, slowly trace the outline of your other hand.

As your finger glides up a finger, inhale through your nose.

As your finger glides down a finger, exhale through your mouth.

Switch hands.

These techniques are just to guide you in noticing your breath. There is no special technique for breathing for toning—only that you do breathe. Inhale before making the sound, and exhale the sound.

2. I Feel Shushed

Have you ever felt "shushed"? As a child, were you told to stop crying? In school, were you told to stop talking or stop laughing, to be quiet? In your teenage years, were you told that your opinions didn't matter? In music class or choir, were you ever told to stand in the back and mouth the words?

I've had some of those experiences and so have my students and clients, leading us to feel that our voices aren't valued and to shut them down for many years.

I was born into a family with two brothers already there. They were very active boys—running around, climbing trees, always on the move. They were so loud and boisterous that I had a hard time getting a word in edgewise. When I was a little older, I saw them get to do whatever they wanted, and I didn't know how to get my needs met. My only solution was to cry. Then I might get my mom's attention. But nobody wanted to hear crying, so I was told to stop.

Were you also told to stop crying?

At the dinner table, I watched my brothers get into lively conversations with our father, who was a Harvard-educated English professor and an alcoholic. Those lively discussions often turned into study sessions, arguments that needed to be backed by research, and eventually some kind of upset with someone leaving the table in a huff. I soon learned that no one's opinion really mattered except the "right" one, which was my father's. Still, I wanted to join those conversations, but at that age I wasn't smart enough to argue my opinions. Even when I was older and could hold my own in a conversation, I was overshadowed by those older brothers. And by then my father was even more frustrated with us as kids, so he was quite harsh with his criticisms of my thought processes. I would feel embarrassed and wish I hadn't even opened my mouth. I learned it was safer to be quiet.

Did you also learn that as a child?

In elementary school, I was basically a good kid. But sometimes other kids would say things that made me laugh. And I would be the one the teacher called out to stop giggling in the back of the classroom. I was so embarrassed to be called out like that. I turned red easily, which caused more people to turn their heads and stare at me. Lesson learned: don't laugh out loud or I'll be embarrassed.

Did you also learn to stop laughing?

In junior high and high school, I loved singing in choir. I was even in the top group as a senior in high school, so I felt like I was pretty good. I loved and revered my high school choir director, so I did what I was told. At one point, he made a point of hushing me. He put his hand up, palm facing me, indicating that I should lower the volume. I did that each time he gave me that signal...until I wasn't making any sound. That's when he gave the "okay" sign. Wow! He didn't want me to make ANY sound! At that time, I got very good at facial expressions and showing the emotions of the music in my body so that even audience members came up to me to compliment me on my performance in the group of singers. And what hurt was that nobody noticed that even in a singing group, my voice was being silenced.

Have you also been silenced in a community of peers where you felt like you belonged—but then began to question yourself after getting the message that your voice wasn't welcome?

I even had my choral conducting professor tell me in a private session that I could not match pitch (the basic musical skill of singing the same tone that's played on a piano). This was at a time when I was preparing to teach children how to sing, which I went on to do for over thirty years. I knew that the professor's criticism wasn't true, but the message still came through loud and clear: I wasn't good enough.

Have you been told negative things about your voice that may or may not be true?

When we're silenced, criticized, or told that our voice isn't welcome, we take it very personally. The voice is a very tender and vulnerable part of us. The anatomy of our throat is made of many strands of tender tissue, not protected by bone or stronger mechanisms around it. So when we're shut down in this area, it can affect our confidence and how we show up in the world. These traumas can cause us to doubt ourselves. They can also cause us to feel fearful. And in our state of fear, we feel we don't deserve to dream of big things for ourselves. We may do what others expect of us and not what we really want to do.

But what would it be like if you could heal your voice? How would it feel to take back the power of your own voice? And what if your voice could heal the traumas you've experienced? Would you feel empowered? Can you even imagine what that would be like?

I felt deeply motivated by discovering the power of my own voice. I discovered the ability to dream big for myself and to believe that I could actually accomplish these dreams. I want that for you as well and for anyone who has felt "less than" because of what happened to disrupt their voice expression.

We can heal our past and move on to a beautiful future filled with all the beauty and joy we can imagine. And that healing can start within us—with our own voice.

Let's Play!

Throughout this book, I invite you to write in a journal, which can take any form you'd like—special book, spiral notebook, digital device, etc. In addition, for the best experience, share with an accountability partner, such as a trusted friend, colleague, or coach/therapist. You may find it helpful to receive this extra support, but this is not absolutely necessary. Let this journey be yours. Allow it to guide you to your best experience.

Journal Play

Take some time to journal about times in your life when you were shushed. By remembering those times, you'll bring them forward to be cleared and healed. You can then replace the difficult memories with soothing new memories. This will give you an entirely new present and future.

Once you've written your stories, imagine what it would have been like if the best situation had happened. For example, in my story of when I was a young child, I might imagine what it would have been like if I'd had quieter brothers who paid attention to me.

Then take that new memory and imagine where you'd be now if that was how it had gone back then. For example, I imagine that if I'd had quieter, kinder brothers who'd paid attention to me, I'd have more confidence in myself. I'd be able to speak more easily because I was being listened to all my life. I wouldn't have had to cry to get what I wanted, and I wouldn't have been shushed.

You can do that with every memory or just test out one or two and spend some time in the new memory.

Then get together with your accountability partner (in person, on the phone, or on Zoom) to share each other's stories. I invite you to listen to each other without giving any advice or suggestions. Just validate each other. Listen and acknowledge that you've heard what they said. You can reply with "thank you." And when the other person is complete, you share with them.

Sound Play

Throughout this book, I'll invite you to make sounds with your voice. Be gentle with yourself, making the sounds in a relaxed manner. Tune in to how they feel in your body. Allow them to ease your nervous system. Find time in your day (starting with just five minutes a day) to add in a Voice Expression practice. Each chapter will focus on one sound. As you are ready, you can start doing the full Voice Expression practice. (You can learn about that at my book extras page: phoebefazio.com/book-extras.)

To help you clear out memories of being shushed and allow the new memories to take hold, you can play with the sound "oh" (as in *home*). This sound can be quite empowering; it's associated with the solar plexus chakra, the energy center of your personal power.

To start, notice how your body feels before you make this sound. Then use your voice to tone the "oh" sound and notice how your body feels as you do that. Do you notice anything shifting? Repeat that for a few breaths. When you're complete with the sounds, how does your body feel?

Play with making that sound, sustaining it and taking breaths as you need to. Focus on your breath as you inhale, then exhale with the sound. As you make the tone, tune in to your upper belly area, just below the rib cage. You can place your hands there to help you feel and focus on that area. If you'd like to imagine the color yellow, the color associated with the solar plexus chakra, that can be powerful as well.

Trust what is happening and really tune in to what you're feeling and sensing. Once you're done, make a note of what you felt before, during, and after the toning. Then share with others how this sound practice felt for you. I encourage you to play with this on a regular basis and notice what's shifting over time.

Playing in Business

The world loves to see the face of your business. Are you shining your light brightly with confidence in your expertise? Are you showing up on video?

If you aren't showing up on video online or doing live in-person talks, maybe it has to do with the idea of feeling shushed. Maybe there's something for you to clear or empower in the solar plexus chakra.

I invite you to go back to your journal and explore this area. And use the sound "oh" as you try the suggestions below. Let this sound soothe you at the solar plexus level and in your energy field.

It can be challenging to show up in the world with your gifts, especially if, like me, you've experienced challenges around performing. So I invite you to use the sound "oh" to soothe your body systems before you make a video or give a talk.

I suggest you hop onto whatever social media you're using and make a thirty-second video. If this is your first video, be vulnerable and let people know that. If you've done videos in the past but currently feel stuck, I recommend letting people know that and sharing that you're coming out of hiding.

If you've been doing videos all along, how can you challenge yourself to take the next step? Let your viewers know that you have something to offer them. (We'll talk more about that when we work on the heart chakra.) Or maybe consider scheduling an in-person talk.

You might try toning the "oh" sound as you prepare to make a video. And if you need soothing afterward, you could do it again.

You might even take a power stance when you make the "oh" sound. For instance, stand with hands on your hips, feet about shoulder distance apart, chest lifted. If you have another power stance that you like, test it out by adding in the toning.

No matter what type of video or in-person talk you choose, be sure to engage your audience. Ask them a question that they can answer yes to. If you post online, ask them to comment below the video. After you tell a story and share what's going on, ask if they've ever experienced that—and invite them to comment. You may need to point down. Many of us need the extra encouragement of the visual.

However you choose to show up in the world, connecting with your voice and your solar plexus chakra will set you up to feel confident as your true self.

3. I'm Afraid to Speak

When I was shushed as a child, I learned to shut down my self-expression, my curiosity, my joy, and also my fear. In fact, I didn't even know I was afraid until I learned how to tune in to the different fear responses (fight, flight, freeze, faint) and move them through my body. Then I felt *all* the fear for a while.

How about you? Do you experience fear, or do you just power through like I used to? If you do feel fear, what's your usual response? Do you want to run? Do you stand up and fight? Do you freeze and get stuck? Or do you feel confused and want to hide under the covers and go back to sleep?

Or perhaps you have different responses at different times. For instance, sometimes I've felt okay about speaking in front of a group, but at other times I've been terrified. Have you had similar experiences?

As a child with a critical, highly educated, alcoholic father and loud older brothers, I felt overshadowed. I worked hard to prove myself in physical ways (like mowing the lawn when I was much too small), but when it came to jumping into a heated argument at the dinner table, I didn't feel like I had anything important to say. If someone did "let me" speak, they'd stare expectantly at me, ready to prove that I really didn't have anything important to say. I would shrink from those stares, feeling like I wasn't worthy. I didn't have what it took. I wasn't enough.

So I became very fearful of saying anything. It was hard for me to ask for help or for something I wanted or needed. When I did ask for something, my mother's response was, "What do you want *that* for?" Often, I didn't feel like I had a good response, so I'd just forget about it.

It took me getting hurt, being very sick, or experiencing a tragedy for my family to come around and offer some care for me. When I cut my foot, my brothers carried me around the campsite. When I was sick with mono in high school, my parents were very concerned for me when I slept all the time. And when my friend was killed and I was crying all the time, my brothers each visited me multiple times and tried to console me.

So, how did I find the courage to speak in public? It started in my sixth-grade speech class. The teacher created a safe environment to speak and showed us how to prepare, so I felt ready for each speech I had to give (even the extemporaneous one where we couldn't prepare). I often felt nervous as I waited for my turn, but once I got up and started talking, I felt good.

As an adult, when I became a teacher, I got used to talking and singing in front of the entire school and at district-wide and all-county events. I enjoyed saying a few words before each song we were going to perform. I even felt safe to stand in front of an audience of students and parents at the honor choir event fully BALD! I had lost my hair during cancer treatments and had worn a hat during the days, but at the evening performance, one of my band-director friends encouraged me to go bald. And I did. I took the opportunity to share about why I was bald, and then went about the business of introducing the directors.

After the concert, a woman told me how much she appreciated me being bald and speaking about cancer, as she was also in treatment for cancer.

Public speaking is often cited as people's worst fear. Many of us do it anyway when it's needed in our jobs, but so many people stay afraid. However, when we can soothe our voice and our nervous system, we may find that speaking gets easier. Our words become clearer, and we're able to express ourselves powerfully and reach people deeply.

Where have you been able to speak with ease? Where have you been afraid to speak? What are you willing to try in order to get better at speaking?

Let's Play!

Journal Play

In your journal, explore any fears you have about speaking in public or talking with other people in small groups or in private. In particular, look at your family. What memories and stories come up for you? Write them down.

After you've written these memories, you can use the technique from the previous chapter to rewrite those memories if you'd like. How do you feel having shifted those memories?

Share as much or as little as you'd like with your accountability partner or in your journal.

Sound Play

Play with the sound "aw," as in the word *tall*. Tune in to your breath as you inhale. As you exhale, make the sound "aaaaawwwwww" sustaining it for as long as is easy. Inhale as needed and, as you exhale, make the sound again. Repeat this for as long as you wish. It's especially helpful to stay with the sound until you feel some kind of a shift.

Tune in to your heart as you make the sound and soothe your heart as you vibrate this area with your voice. The heart is where we connect with others and are of service. When we tune in to our hearts as we speak, we allow ourselves to connect on a deeper, more vulnerable level, and we allow others to feel us.

What did you feel as you made the "aw" sound? What shifted for you? Please share with your accountability partner or in your journal.

Playing in Business

The way I see the chakras in business, the heart chakra is aligned with your program and what you offer to the world. If you're offering your services in the typical healing/medical scenario (client comes in and lies on your table, you do your work on them, they leave), then I encourage you to consider something a little different.

Consider the greater transformation you offer your clients. What can you offer over a longer time with them? If you've never considered this, it could take some time to work out a program to offer. With this approach, you can offer your clients something life changing that they can't get from seeing you for one session at a time.

No matter what you offer—single sessions, packages of sessions, or a bigger program—let's use this time to discuss HOW you're offering your services.

Is it difficult for you to offer your work to people, even when you know you can help them? Do you stumble over the words? Do you freeze and later think of what you could have said?

Let's use your journal again here. As you make the sound of "aw" to soothe your heart, feel into your heart space and remember that you've been given healing gifts for a reason. (The Divine didn't give you these gifts and then leave you hanging!) In a different chapter, we'll talk about connecting to the Divine with your voice, but for now, start by tuning in to your heart.

As you do this, think of one client at a time. Feel your connection with them and tune in to what they're coming to you for, what they're needing or wanting in their life right now that you have the solution for. Write about how you could offer your services to them.

How would it feel to speak to them like that? Before you do this, maybe you'll have to go back to the exercises above and clear away some old painful memories. This healing work will greatly assist you with speaking to your clients about how you can help them. Continue to make the sounds and soothe your heart. Trust in this process. You definitely have something that people want and need.

We'll go deeper into this later in the book.

4. I Can't Sing

Was there a time that you stopped singing? Or has it been hard for you to sing? Were you ever told that you "couldn't" or "shouldn't" sing? Or did you feel like you couldn't or shouldn't?

I don't remember when I started to sing or how it sounded, but I do have vague memories of being outside and making sounds with my voice when I was very young. And I remember that when I was "singing," I felt free. At some point, when I was around two years old, someone said something, and for a long time, I was too embarrassed to sing.

Years later, when I found my voice again, I remembered the positive feelings I'd felt during my early years. It was like coming home to a familiar place that I'd long abandoned. Once again I was able to experience freedom through my voice.

In elementary school I loved singing around the piano while the teacher played. There was no judgment. Just singing for fun. No one told us how to sing or how not to sing. No one even seemed to be listening to us. We just sang from our hearts. It felt free and easy.

As I went up in the grades, I continued to enjoy singing in groups. In choir I felt hugged by all the other voices around me. My voice joined with other people's voices. Sometimes it felt like I had no individual voice, as together we were one voice. At other times, I could hear different voices around me as well as my own. The more voices, the easier it was for me to feel free.

Whenever the opportunity for a solo came up, I longed to try out, and I envied those who did, but for years I was too afraid. In high school and in college, I finally summoned the courage to audition for the top-level choir. Despite the disappointment of not making it on the first try, I came back and eventually made it in. But I still didn't sing solos.

Singing at home as a child was a different story, though. My brothers and I would sing along with our records. Sometimes my oldest brother and I would sing together, and he tried to show me how to sing in harmony—he sang one part while I sang a different part. We never seemed very happy with how that sounded, though, which made me feel less than. I didn't think I could sing the way I was told to, so I was that much more afraid to sing alone. (As it turned out, I was the one with the musical ear, while he's never been very successful with his music!)

Even though I had success in choirs, I still had this sense that I couldn't sing. Have you ever felt that way? If so, I'm happy to share that there's good news on this topic, so keep reading!

After years of teaching vocal music in schools as well as private voice lessons, I've come to realize some of the challenges with singing that many of us face. For instance:

- We have the idea that we need to sound like our favorite professional singers.
- We may not be able to hear our own voice.
- It can take practice to match pitch.
- Sometimes the words get in the way.
- Rhythm can be confusing.

But these very things that can make it hard to sing are some of the reasons why I love the idea of toning. It's not singing, but it involves making sound with your voice. No words, no pitch to match, no rhythm, and no need for years of training in order to do it.

Toning is very different from singing, yet it can sometimes look, feel, and sound like singing. We'll go into that later. Right now, just open your mind to the idea that there's a way to make sound with your voice that's healing and can't be done wrong. How does that sound?

If you've been injured emotionally around your singing voice, then this is probably good news. If not, this could be something new for you to play with and explore.

Let's Play!

Journal Play

In your journal, write about your experiences with singing. Take a look at your younger years, before school, during your early school years, and through high school and college. What did you experience regarding singing? Do you have happy memories? Or were there times when someone told you not to sing? Was there a teacher or parent or sibling or friend who said things that caused you to stop singing?

Share with your accountability partner or in your journal about your experiences with singing.

How does it feel after you share these memories with others? Do you feel a bit lighter? Or is it upsetting to remember those times?

Remember that with any difficult memories, you can play with creating something new. What if that went a different way? Imagine a positive way and play it out. Who would you be now if the new memory is what you experienced? (See the "Journal Play" section in Chapter 2 for more ideas on this.)

Sound Play

After doing the writing and remembering what singing was like for you, you can use the sound of "oo" (as in *soothe*) to nourish yourself.

The "oo" sound is associated with the sacral chakra. This is the part of the body where the womb is located. This is the seat of creativity and creation. As you create new memories, tap into this energy center to help with birthing the new experience.

Tuning in and placing your hands gently on the lower belly, inhale fully, and at the top of that inhale, exhale the sound "oo." Sustain the "oo" sound until you desire another inhale. Allow the next inhale to refill you. Then, on the top of that next inhale, exhale again the sound of "oo." Continue this until you feel complete. You may notice a shift in your body or your awareness. Stay open to notice these subtle changes.

As you complete this sound practice, allow yourself to enjoy the silence that follows. And when you feel ready, go ahead and write about that experience. What did you notice? What came to you? Did you find comfort and relaxation? Or did it spark something and ignite something fiery in you?

Share with your accountability partner or in your journal about what you're experiencing. Putting it into words can help with your expression in other ways.

Playing in Business

The sacral chakra in business aligns with your ideal clients. And since the sacral chakra is your money center, you can keep in mind that your clients are also the flow of income to you. If money is a challenging energy for you, then focus more on the client. You get to design and attract this ideal client. The sacral chakra being all about creation, this is where you get to unleash your inner creator.

Who is your ideal client? What do you know about this person?

What do they need or want? What problem do they have that you can help solve? The more you can tune in to the exact nature of this problem and how it's affecting their life, the more you'll be able to show them how your solution will get them what they want and need.

Remember to choose someone you enjoy serving, as you'll be attracting lots more like them! And remember that you have the solution for their problem. Your healing gifts are exactly what they need.

Get out your journal again and start writing. Do some more toning of the "oo" sound so that you can connect to your creative energy center. Allow the sounds to be playful. I often notice that my voice wants to make different sounds with "oo." Sometimes it becomes almost song-like. Other times I feel something new about the sound and the focus on the lower abdomen.

Write about how it feels to make the "oo" sound. Then write about one client you help. Describe them in as much detail as you can and get very specific about the problem they have. What is it? How bad is it for them? How ready are they to let it go? Get into their head and describe their experience in as much detail as you can.

If you haven't worked with any clients yet, you can do this exercise by talking with people. It's great to get on a call with them and ask them about what they feel challenged with in their life. Ask them what they've tried before and what they'd pay to have relief from this problem. You may be surprised at what you can learn.

Take really good notes in their exact words. Those words are very important as we begin to talk about this with others. This is quite magical. When you speak to someone about their problem in their own words, they feel like you understand them, and they'll be more ready to hear you when you say you can help them.

Be careful not to sell them anything on that call, though. At that point, you're just gathering information. If they lean in and want your help, I recommend getting on another call later. That call can be more about what it might look like to get your help for their problem.

Use the sounds to tune in. We'll do more of this later in the book to get even clearer about who your ideal client is, so don't worry if you didn't get very far. But test it out.

Use your journal to describe who your client is. Using the questions above, spend time creating a profile of this person.

5. I Can't Perform

Have you decided that you can't perform? Do you get nervous just thinking about doing anything in front of an audience? Are there some things you easily do in front of an audience and other things that you feel you could NEVER do?

Long ago I decided, *I'm not very good at performing. I get too nervous*. In college I wondered, *How am I going to be a piano performance major if I'm too nervous to perform?* I knew I'd have to perform for exams in order to complete my degree. When it was time for me to declare a major, I wanted to major in music, but the only way I felt I could do this was to play the piano. I thought about singing, but that felt even harder, as I had no formal training (or so I thought). I thought the only way I could major in music with my voice was to sing solo. And since I was too afraid to sing by myself, I thought that was out.

I knew I'd have to get a handle on my performance anxiety, so I took my dad's advice to go to the counseling center and see if I could get some help. They directed me to the "Relaxation Room" to learn how to calm myself so I wouldn't be too nervous. I also met with a counselor on a weekly basis and even did a few groups such as "assertiveness training," which helped me in all areas of my life.

In addition, I watched other music majors perform and spoke with them about how they overcame performance anxiety. That didn't help much, though, as the ones who shared techniques with me already had the nerves figured out or just didn't get as nervous as I did. They seemed to have no problem performing from memory, whereas whenever I tried this, my mind would go blank and I couldn't remember what I was supposed to be playing.

My piano teacher in college recommended that I perform regularly in order to get better at performing. That made sense. We had lots of opportunities to perform something short at lunchtime recitals. So every time I learned a short piece or a part of a piece (one movement, for example), I would sign up to perform it. The audience was small, but we played in the recital hall on the big grand piano, so it felt just like those scary recitals from years past.

I learned a lot from those practice recitals. I watched other pianists for specific ways they played. Some moved their bodies, using their hands and arms in a way that was different from how I played. I watched every nuance, from the way they walked out on stage to how they adjusted the bench and how they placed their hands on the keyboard.

The biggest lesson I learned came as I waited backstage for my turn. The stagehands would usually be goofing off out of boredom, as they didn't have much to do. They made me laugh. This meant that I was already laughing when I walked out on stage. That helped lighten my mood and allowed me to relax a bit. But making mistakes still troubled me. Perfectionism.

The best thing I learned for overcoming perfectionism was how to start off imperfectly. I attribute this to some of the silliness that happened backstage. One time when we were joking around, I shared about how nervous I always felt. The guy backstage asked me what I was nervous about. I replied that I was most afraid of making a mistake. So he jokingly suggested I pretend to trip on the way out.

I tried that. It made me laugh and relax. I realized that since I'd already made a mistake (by tripping), then I wouldn't have to worry about other mistakes. There are bound to be mistakes, but the first one is always the scariest, isn't it?

I've used this technique for every performance I've done since then. I would sometimes plan the first mistake, and sometimes I'd discover where the mistake was. For instance, I might decide not to shave my legs, or I might forget to do something I always do before I perform. Or I would trip on my way out. There was always something I could do that felt like a mistake so I wouldn't have to worry about making that first mistake on stage. This calmed me as I got ready, letting go of the stress of doing everything just the way I wanted it to be done, and somehow it eased the pressure of having a perfect performance.

Have you ever struggled with performing? Do you also struggle with perfectionism? What techniques have you used to address these struggles?

Why am I talking about performing in a book about voice and vision? We don't have to perform on stage in order to heal our voice or tap into our vision. However, many of us connect the voice with singing and with performing. And there's something about performing that goes beyond being on stage. And it's very important.

Let's Play!

Journal Play

Write in your journal:

- Are there areas of your life where you feel like you're performing?
- Do you get worried about making it perfect?
- How could you use this idea of being imperfect before you start in order to ease the tension of feeling like you have to perform perfectly?

Sound Play

Let's tune in to the brow chakra (between the eyebrows) with the sound "eye." This energy center is where we receive our visions. So I invite you to allow yourself to "see" yourself performing in any way that looks and feels good for you.

Tuning in and placing your hands on your forehead, inhale fully with ease, and at the top of that full inhale, exhale the sound of "eye." Sustain this sound as long as it lasts, and as your desire to refill arrives, go ahead and allow yourself to be filled again. At the top of that next inhale, allow the sound of "eye" to resonate again. And continue with this process until you feel a sense of completion.

We'll spend more time later with this chakra energy as we tap into your vision in the Visioning Process. For now, notice how it feels to vibrate this part of your body.

Note in your journal how it felt. What showed up for you? What did you feel? See? Hear? Know? Sense?

When we put words to our experience, especially our vision, we're taking action to bring it into reality. There's much more on this in future visioning chapters, but for now, share your experiences with an accountability partner.

Playing in Business

The brow chakra is related to your vision for your business. Having a clear idea of what your business will look and feel like is key to knowing what your next steps are.

What's the highest vision for your healing work in the world? If you don't know yet, that's okay. We'll focus a lot more on vision in the coming sections, including the Visioning Process, which will guide you toward your highest vision. This vision will have information for you to tap into, so you'll be able to discover your next steps.

For now, take some time to write down what you see for your business.

- What's the structure of your business?
- How many clients would you like to have?
- How much money would you like to make each month?
- How often do you want to work?

Be creative and don't let the "how" get in the way. Our minds like to stop us by saying things like, "You can't do it that way" or "Why would you want to do that?" Acknowledge those thoughts and keep designing.

Use your voice here. Make the "eye" sound, and as you feel the vibration between your eyes, imagine your business ideas and the perfect life you'd like to live. What elements of your business and your life could you start to bring in now?

Use your journal or speak with your accountability partner about what you'll bring into your life that could move you even one step closer to your vision.

6. How Can I Feel Safe Exploring Sound?

In this book, I've been inviting you to use your voice to make unusual sounds. I understand how intimidating that might feel if you've never done it before.

Do you worry about other people hearing your sounds? Does this fear stand in your way of being able to fully embody sounds and their vibrations? Is this what keeps you from making these sounds with your voice?

Me too. I've always been self-conscious of my singing or sounding. Sometimes I'm even self-conscious about talking.

So, let's explore places and spaces that not only create a sense of safety but also a feeling of adventure.

The safest place I've found for me to do my daily Voice Expression practice is in the car. Alone. I used to drop the kids off at school and then do my vocalizing in the car on the way to work. Now, after ten years of making these sounds on a daily basis, I still do my Voice Expression practice alone in the car.

The car is a great place for various reasons. The main one is that you're alone and no one can hear you. It's like a moving practice room. The other cool thing is that because there are so many windows in a car, there's an effect where the sound bounces off the windows. So listen carefully to extra sounds and feel the extra vibrations. You may have already experienced this without realizing what was happening. I was hearing high-pitched, whistle-like sounds at times, and it wasn't until I read about the way sound bounces off glass that I realized why it felt so magical in the car.

Remember, no radio. This is exploring time for you and your own voice.

Also, safety note: don't close your eyes while you're driving. You can pull over and do this practice in the car without driving. Then you could go deeper into meditation with eyes closed. I have, at times, gone out to the car to do my practice without driving, especially when I know I won't have alone time while driving, like on a road trip with others.

Bathrooms are also fantastic for acoustics that create more sounds and a more expansive sensation of your voice. The sound waves bounce off the tiles and mirrors, creating more sensations and interesting sound experiences. The shower has been identified by many people as a place to sing, so this is the same idea. Play with facing the corner of the shower and notice how that feels versus facing away from the corner into the open space.

Any place in nature is also wonderful for making sounds. I live on a dirt road with lots of trees. When I walk on my road, I like to do my Voice Expression practice outside with the trees. I breathe in their wonderful oxygen and feel the cycling of me sharing my carbon dioxide for them. I see my Voice Expression practice as a gift to the trees. They're so playful with me and so appreciative of my singing.

I also love making sounds near or in water. I love the white-noise sensation of running water, as in a river or creek, as well as the sound of waves crashing and receding on the sand. Even running water in the sink or bathtub can make it easy to make sound. The combination of white noise and negative ions supports us as we step into a tender area of making sound with our own voice—sounds that might turn heads if others heard us. I can feel comfortable out in nature at a creek, even if I know that people may be walking by. The calming, soothing sound and feel of the running water lets me feel good and not at all concerned about anyone hearing me.

What type of nature do you have around you? How does it feel to make sound outside in nature? Notice what you feel and hear when you make sounds in nature. Is it easier for you? Or are you more concerned about other people hearing you?

Try making sounds in any of the places mentioned above. Or, if you're feeling adventurous, try making sounds underneath bridges, in stairwells, inside hollow trees, in caves, or anywhere else you feel safe. Wherever you discover your safe place, open your heart to the sounds that want to come through you. When I feel that the sound is channeling through me, rather than me generating the sounds, then I'm able to let go of the sense that I'm the one creating and performing the sounds. This allows me to let go of the fear of what other people think.

Whether you're making the exact sounds of the Voice Expression practice or exploring different sounds, I encourage you to play. Explore. Go adventuring. Have fun.

Let's Play!

Journal Play

Write in your journal:

- In which of the places mentioned above do you feel safe making sounds?
- Where have you been going to make your sounds so far?
- Not feeling able to make the sounds yet? Write about those feelings.

Pick one place and test it out. Then do it daily to keep the practice going. It will get easier. Notice the changes you experience each time you do it.

What are some other places you want to try? Did you think of some that aren't mentioned here?

Share with your accountability partner or write more about it in your journal.

Sound Play

To help you feel more grounded, no matter where you choose to make sound, let's connect to the root chakra by making the sound "uh" (as in *love*). Inhale, then exhale while sustaining this sound. Tune in to the base of your spine, your legs, your feet, and the soles of your feet as they connect to the earth. If you're seated, feel the connection of your seat as you connect to the chair or directly on the earth.

Allow yourself to relax more as you continue to inhale and exhale the sound of "uh." Notice your shoulders letting go. Notice your face muscles relaxing. Feel your jaw hanging loosely and your tongue resting on the bottom of your mouth. Continue making this sound and feeling the vibrations until you feel a shift or you feel complete.

Share in your journal, with your accountability partner, or in your community:

- How did it feel to make this sound and connect to the earth?
- Did you feel a shift?
- Were you able to relax?
- Did you feel more grounded?

Playing in Business

The root chakra coordinates with your platform for your business.

Where are you standing and grounding into so that you can share your message to the world?

Online this could be social media platforms or emails, blogs, or websites. In real life, it could be where you give talks or other places where you meet people. There are many options. And it can be overwhelming to think we have to be on all of them.

If you're feeling overwhelmed by all the possibilities related to your business platform, I suggest you spend some extra time with the sound of "uh." Nice and low and relaxed. Connect with the earth. Tune in to your ideal clients. Ask to be guided to where they're showing up. If you aren't sure, a good place to start is on Facebook. Many people are on that platform, and most of us are able to use it in various ways.

If you haven't been on Facebook, start with a personal profile. Set that up and find the people you know. Look up friends and family, then start sharing. Share a mix of personal and business posts. In fact, on Facebook it's best to make only one out of every three posts for your work. The other two are personal. Share something from your life—your pets, your adventures, even your struggles. Being vulnerable is real and helps people get to know you.

If you're already on a different social media platform, then keep going with that. See if you're already doing the one-in-three manner of posting.

If you don't use social media and you feel that your clients won't be there either, then you'll want to show up live somewhere. Consider leading healing circles or gatherings of your ideal clients, or giving a talk to share some great info for your clients to use without purchasing anything. Then it can be a nice next step to offer a call or a session to help them further.

Email is an essential part of any business, even if social media is where your people are and they're finding you. Social media platforms can change, and you could lose your potential clients, so always grow your email list. I share more about how to do that in my trainings and coaching, but it can be as simple as asking people if they'd like to join your list whenever you're talking and they seem interested in what you're sharing.

This is a huge topic. So if you find yourself in overwhelm and shutdown, come back to your voice. Make the "uh" sound. And keep it simple, focusing on one step at a time, one client at a time. What's the next step for you? Where's your next client going to find you? Try to stay in one place so they can find you easily.

7. I'm Not Expressing Myself the Way I Want To

Have you become aware of the throat chakra being an issue for you? Is that one reason you were drawn to read this book? What have you discovered already about your concern with your throat chakra? What are you hoping to shift?

The physical mechanism of speaking is in our throat. The throat is made up of a network of tendons and very little bone structure. Spine at the back, hyoid in the front, nothing to shield this tender area. This is a very narrow part of our body, yet it's where we carry an immense amount of power. And also vulnerability.

When the throat chakra is balanced and the energy flows easily, we're able to express ourselves with a graceful power (e.g., by speaking our truth with love, saying what we mean, sharing from the heart), but when this chakra is out of balance, we can feel unable to speak, write, or communicate our needs and wants to others. Or we can be overly expressive (e.g., yelling, oversharing, talking over others).

There are many ways we can lose that precious balance, such as through physical or emotional trauma, fear, anger, or grief. And we can quickly go in and out of balance in a moment.

Some say that the arms and hands are a part of the throat chakra energy as well. So when we move the energy with our hands and arms, we can facilitate the balancing of the throat chakra.

Probably the most powerful way to balance and align our throat chakra energy is to make sound. If words don't come, we can hum or make any type of sound. (Animal sounds are fun!) Singing along to a favorite song (without judging yourself) is helpful. Or you can ask yourself what emotion you're feeling and what sound that makes.

When we add intention to the sounds we make with our voice, we create a powerful practice. If you want to shift an emotion from negative to positive, for instance, you can stay with that sound until the shift occurs on its own. Sometimes the emotion will flow out in tears or body movements that express it even more fully.

A great healer taught me that all healing begins with balancing and aligning the chakras and the energy system. Once these are aligned, our body can begin to heal itself, which is the aim of most energy healing work.

What if you made a sound for each of your chakras every day and you had the intention to bring yourself into alignment and balance? What if you tuned in to the vibration and sensations you felt as you did that? What could your body heal in the process?

Through this practice, I discovered that my body, mind, and soul became aligned. My body stayed healthy and began the deep healing of childhood wounds and even past-life experiences, bloodlines, and my heritage. I began to receive divine messages on a regular basis.

I also noticed that I was able to speak more clearly and in a way that people were listening to me more. And because I felt so grounded in myself, I didn't feel the embarrassment that I used to feel when I was younger. I felt safe to talk about things that might seem unusual for most people—things like channeling and sound healing. I could even stand in front of an audience and make "weird sounds" and hear what people had to say about how those sounds felt to them. I wasn't embarrassed or triggered in any way.

Instead, I realized that these "weird sounds" were channeled messages from other healing beings for the specific healing of anyone who was listening. And when I added these sounds to my Reiki sessions, clients felt amazing results. (More about that later.)

Let's Play!

Journal Play

Write in your journal on the topic of the throat chakra:

- Have you ever noticed issues with your throat chakra before? Have you had trouble expressing yourself?

- How does your throat feel after reading about this chakra?
- What would you like to shift with regard to your throat chakra?
- Are you feeling a desire to make some sound to support your throat chakra?

After you write, share your ahas with your accountability partner.

Sound Play

Let's play with the sound associated with the throat chakra—"ay" (as in *say*).

Take a deep breath and then exhale this sound for as long as you can easily sustain it. At the end of your exhale, allow the air to come back in naturally. Then, as you exhale, repeat the sound. Continue until you feel something shift or change in your body, mind, or spirit. Be gentle here. No need to push the sound. Allow it to come out without judgment. As you feel more at ease, you may notice the sound becoming stronger, more expansive. If that doesn't happen, don't let it worry you. Just take note of what you're experiencing.

In your journal, describe your experiences and answer these questions:

- How did your throat feel before making sound?
- How did it feel during your sound creation?
- How did you feel afterward?

- Was this a difficult experience?
- Did it bring up fears or other emotions?

You might consider giving yourself time for writing anything else that comes to mind that wants to be expressed. When we activate this chakra, we may find we have a lot to express that's been stuck. And it may have been stuck for a very long time, so let yourself express whatever comes out.

As you feel safe, share with your accountability partner and then connect with others about your experiences with the throat chakra.

Playing in Business

The throat is our expression, so if we're not aligned with our throat, we may have trouble talking about what we do and how we help people. If you're struggling with that, then focus on the "ay" sound.

The throat is sometimes a bit elusive when we try to go directly to it. If we work only on the throat, then it can work against us. It can easily become overworked, which creates more challenges. So, as you tune in to what comes up for you around speaking about your work—in one-on-one conversations, group talks, or videos—you may notice an issue with your throat. If this is the case, make the "ay" sound and write about it in your journal.

Keep doing all of the sounds. As we make the sounds of the chakras with our own voice, we're strengthening our vocal mechanism. Use the sound of your stronger chakras to soothe the throat. Bring up your heart energy by toning the "aw" sound, then move to the "ay" sound of the throat. This is a powerful way to support any of your struggling chakras.

If you've been resisting making videos or talking about your healing work and how it helps others, I encourage you to commit to doing the Voice Expression practice on a regular basis. Then see how it feels to write about it in your journal or share with your accountability partner.

8. I Want to Express Myself Clearly and Powerfully

If you've had any kind of trauma related to your voice, then you have some healing to do. And let's face it, who hasn't had some kind of trauma to their voice? For instance, have you had times when you spoke but people couldn't hear your message? Have you ever been embarrassed by using your voice? Or, as we discussed earlier, have you been shushed?

I shared before that I started counseling to help me with my severe stage fright. Although I wasn't performing with my voice at that time, the counseling did help me heal my voice, as I was able to share about my childhood and release some of the secrets I hadn't known I'd been carrying. In those sessions I learned a lot about my childhood that I hadn't seen before, like that my dad was an alcoholic. I thought I had a "normal" childhood. I thought others experienced similar things. It was painful to my parents when I shared what I was learning about myself in my sessions. I couldn't express myself very well to my mother, who I felt was a bit abusive—mostly through neglect—and I was still healing from my own trauma.

It would be many years later—when I needed to go back to counseling—that I began the real voice healing. As I described in the introduction, it all began in sessions with an energy healer who was also a psychotherapist. Before those sessions, I didn't realize my throat had so much healing to do.

At that time I was shifting from a logical, pragmatic way of living to a spiritually guided, free-flowing way of living. As my voice was healing, my heart was opening, the veil was being pulled back, and I was surrendering to something familiar at a soul level yet so unfamiliar to me in this lifetime.

The rest of the voice healing came while I did my daily Voice Expression practice and my Sound Washing® (more about this later). I was guided to this practice because I didn't know what I was going to do with this newfound voice. I was told in my meditations to "just do it." So, to try to "just do it," I chose a daily practice of toning my chakras with my voice, which became my Voice Expression practice. I would do this practice in the car every day after dropping the kids off at school, followed by some Sound Washing.

Because I didn't have a lot of spare time then, I only dedicated about five to ten minutes a day to this practice. But the important part was that I fit it into my day.

How about you?

- Do you feel that your voice could use some healing?
- Do you want to be able to speak more clearly? Or to sing—alone or with a group?
- Would you like to use your own voice to heal and align your voice and your life?
- How will you heal your voice?

If you'd like to try the Voice Expression practice, that's available at my book extras page: phoebefazio.com/book-extras. I suggest that you begin with short sessions and set up a time of day that allows you to be consistent. It takes commitment to really do it on a daily basis, but I've found that it's well worth it. So have my clients.

For instance, before I worked with Cathy, she couldn't show up on video without crying or breaking into a sweat. However, after a few months of doing the Voice Expression practice regularly (with me and on her own), she was able to record and post a video with ease and grace.

When I started working with Gail, she was struggling to grow her psychic medium business online. After a few sessions with me and doing the Voice Expression practice and visioning, she met and began channeling the collective known as the "Soul's Collective," and her business took off.

Kerry was busy working on her coaching business while holding down another job and raising her daughter alone, which gave her little time to play her violin. After a few sessions with me and practicing the Voice Expression practice, she reconnected to this love of playing violin, and over the next year she added in the cello and even began teaching local kids how to play violin.

These results are just a few examples of the power of your own voice to heal your voice. The Voice Expression practice I use and teach is simple, but over time it can be deeply healing. I encourage you to check it out.

Let's Play!

Journal Play

By now, you may be getting the hang of writing about your experiences in your journal, so let's dive in with a bit of introspection:

- How has it felt for you to play with making these sounds with your voice?
- What are you feeling—emotionally, physically, and spiritually?
- What struggles are you noticing? Do you feel resistance? Fears?
- What do you need to know that would make this easier?
- What are you celebrating for yourself?

Explore these topics by yourself or with your accountability partner.

Sound Play

If you haven't started doing the full Voice Expression practice yet, you can find all the resources at my book extras page (for URL, see "Contact Information" at the end of this book), which includes a how-to video, an audio version, and a colored chart for all seven major chakras.

In this full practice, you'll be making a sound for each of these chakras one at a time. Once you get the hang of it, you can do it daily. The more you practice it, the easier it becomes. You may even memorize it, which will free you up to do it anywhere.

I recommend you download the audio track to your favorite listening device and take it to your safe space for making sound. And set up a time to do it daily so it becomes a habit.

Take note in your journal how you feel before, during, and after each session. And be sure to share your experiences with your accountability partner and in your community.

Keep reading to discover more chakras as part of the twelve-chakra system.

Playing in Business

This seven-chakra Voice Expression practice is very powerful for you and your business. By practicing this every day (even for as little as five minutes), you'll notice your voice shifting, strengthening, clearing, softening, and opening. What word describes what you're experiencing?

As you continue this practice every day, you'll find more ease with it. You can tune in to each part of your business as you do that. To help you visualize the chakras, the colors, and how they show up for your business, please see the chart "7 Proven Steps to Grow Your Healing Business Online" (Appendix C).

Another helpful tool for you is the seven-day challenge where we can do the Voice Expression practice together for seven days. My clients enjoy doing this practice along with me whenever we can. It feels a little different than when we do it alone. They're both great, but it's nice to have some variety and connection. If you're interested in the seven-day challenge, look for it on the book extras page.

We'll be using this practice as well as the twelve-chakra version that's coming up later with the Visioning Process.

Share in your journal about this practice and how it's going for you. Take note of any resistance you're experiencing about doing this or other things that can move your business forward. Perhaps discussing with your business coach or colleagues would be beneficial.

9. Do I Have to Be a Soloist?

Do you ever feel like you can't sing because you don't have the voice of one of your favorite professional singers? Do you feel like singing in a group would be just as hard as singing by yourself?

I used to be very afraid to sing solo. I loved singing in groups, though. There were opportunities to try out for solos in those groups, but I never felt safe enough or good enough to try out.

In our society, soloists are considered the gold standard of singing. They're the divas, the celebrities, the revered ones. Yet I've always preferred singing in a choir. I love hearing my voice resonating with others, blending with them so that my voice almost disappears, feeling all the vibrations holding me and joining with me. Whether we're all singing the same notes, harmonizing, or even singing dissonant sounds together, the experience is transcendent. And we don't have a choir unless we have a group of people!

Have you felt this sense of belonging?

In my many years as a choir director, I've developed a deep appreciation for all the voices coming together. But I felt this even before I had words for it. I remember in high school feeling tired and not wanting to go to choir class, then leaving class feeling rejuvenated and joyful after an hour of singing and vibrating together.

Performing in a choir was much more fun for me than doing anything solo, like playing the piano. Within the parameters of the music and the structure of the group, I felt free to show emotion on my face and in my body language. I felt like an important part of something bigger—much like how I feel being a spiritual being in this human experience with all of you on this planet at this time.

Although much of what we'll be doing here is about making our own sounds, I encourage you to find trusted friends to join in the magic of a group sound experience. Whenever you feel ready—either now or after you've been making these sounds for a while on your own—you might start with one person. Later, you can invite others to join in. You may find that people want to come together and make sound on a regular basis. Call it a toning circle or a sound gathering. Get creative. You might eventually add in some instruments, but I find it even more powerful when we stay with just our voices. Sometimes the instruments can be a distraction. Other times, however, they're a nice addition that gives our voices time to rest, and they can add an element that opens up the creativity of the group.

Let's Play!

Journal Play

In your journal, answer these questions:

- Have you ever sung in a group setting, such as at church, in a choir, or during family gatherings?
- If not, what has stopped you?
- Would you like to join with others to experience sound in a new way?
- Are you willing to try a new experience?
- If you have sung with a group, how did it feel?
- Does singing create sacred space for you?

Sound Play

If you've been experimenting with your voice as you read this book, congratulations. If not, I understand. It can be uncomfortable.

In either case, here's something that can help you take your sound play to the next level: I invite you to reach out to others and invite them to join you in something you've been playing with. Or, if you haven't yet started to play with sounds on your own, maybe asking others to join you will give you courage.

When you invite people into a group setting to make sounds together, let it be playful. Assure them that no one will judge them.

You may be pleasantly surprised by the number of people who want to join you. And the sounds may be so transformative that you can't go without it.

See where it takes you. What new ideas and awareness come? Follow the energy and the guidance that shows up.

Although this is best done in person, it can also work via online video conferencing platforms such as Zoom.

If you don't want to start your own group, you could look on Meetup. Search for toning groups already happening near you. You might be surprised to find one.

To give you something to do for your sound practice (solo or in a group), let's tap into the crown chakra with the sound "ee" (as in *free*). The color violet is associated with this chakra. So call in the purple and feel the top of your head as you inhale, expanding with ease. Then exhale the sound "ee." Sustain as long as it feels good, then inhale again and continue the sound on the next exhale.

Feel the unconditional love of the Divine flow into you through this chakra. Allow this "ee" to invite the flow of divine love into your being. Feel it flow in and through your entire being and connect you to the earth.

Take as much time as you'd like to spend with this beautiful sensation.

Then, whenever you're ready, share in your journal or with your accountability partner how it feels to make the sound of the Divine and to invite in unconditional love.

Playing in Business

The crown chakra in our business is our practice. Since the crown is traditionally our connection to the Divine, this practice can be one of your spiritual practices. (As a healer, you probably have many.)

While spiritual practices are essential, so are business practices—the specific skills that will help us build and grow our business, such as practicing being on video or practicing writing for your website or social media in a way that attracts clients and gives them helpful tips. This is how they'll get to know you. And as they do, they'll begin to trust you and eventually will want to buy from you. They'll feel your divine connection and be drawn to you.

Those of us who are more sensitive need to practice saying (or writing) the words, as they don't always come naturally to us. Toning and sound play can help with this.

As you call on the Divine with the sound "ee," you may want to explore a bit with the energy of the Divine. I invite you to allow your voice to float higher and noodle around with the upper tones. As you float up there with your voice, you may feel a beautiful connection with the Divine. You may feel the support and unconditional love that can soothe you as you practice the tools and strategies of building a business.

Make the sounds, then describe the experience in your journal or to your accountability partner.

II. Visioning and Sound: Discovering Your Highest Vision

1. What Is Visioning and How Do I Do It?

"When your thoughts and actions begin to align with the imperatives of your soul, you enroll the full support of the universe. Unimagined possibilities begin to open up as you synchronize with the divine."
– Michael Bernard Beckwith

Have you done a Visioning Process before? Do you create vision boards? Do you spend time designing the life you most desire?

The Visioning Process I've used in various situations is one where I go into a meditative state and ask God/Spirit/Source what They would like me to see in this moment. What's my highest vision? What will guide me toward the purpose for my being?

I've done this in groups to support my spiritual center and also with my clients who are feeling called to grow their healing businesses. It's a profound practice of asking and receiving.

Sometimes we're given a vision that's unexpected. Sometimes the same vision comes up for each question. Sometimes we get lots of clear details, and other times it seems confusing.

When I'm guiding the visioning, I remind people that we don't all "see" the vision. It may come as a knowing or a feeling, or we may see glimpses and pieces of a larger vision.

I encourage them to take the time while they're in the vision to see and feel the details. Are you inside or outside? Are you alone? What are you wearing? Look around and even behind you, which is sometimes very interesting.

With this type of visioning practice, we can return for details we forgot to look for before. And we can ask questions like *How did I get here?*, *What steps did I take?*, and *What's my reason for being here?*

My most memorable vision is one where I was standing on stage with the lights shining on me. I was dressed up with my hair and makeup looking amazing, and I was speaking to a packed audience in a small theater, much like a local theater near me. It felt familiar. The audience was very excited by what I was sharing, and I knew I had family and friends backstage supporting me as well.

The one question I couldn't seem to get an answer to was *What am I speaking about?* I visited my vision many times and still couldn't get clear on it. Was I telling my story? Was I performing my Sound Washing? Was I teaching? If so, what was I teaching? Was I facilitating a workshop?

Not long after receiving that vision, I saw images of my mentor doing exactly what I saw myself doing. I was drawn to work with her. As I learned from her, I discovered what I was speaking about and how to get my message out there. Now I have found myself on the stage—although not in front of such a full audience yet, but I know I'm on my way. What I also know now is that I'm speaking to people about their voice and their vision—and how they can use their voice to live their vision of a profitable, sustainable healing business. Perhaps I'm speaking about this book!

Let's Play!

Journal Play

I recommend starting with the Voice Expression practice for the seven chakras, as it brings the body and mind into a beautifully receptive state. (You can find all the details on the book extras page—URL at end of book.)

Once in the state of receiving information, you will go into a meditation.

You can read the complete guided meditation in the next chapter, but here is the basic idea:

You will ask your highest guidance to show you your highest vision in a way that you'll understand. What's the vision for you to see now that will help you move forward with your purpose here on earth at this time?

Take whatever images show up. Say yes to what you see and look for the *and*, just like comedy improv players who play the game "Yes, and." Ask your questions to get more clarity. Look around. Take it all in. Try not to doubt yourself or ask how this is going to happen.

After the meditation, I recommend taking time to write down every detail from this vision. Even if you don't "see" anything in the meditation, start writing and explore what comes. Maybe you felt something or had a knowing that something or someone was there. Tune in to what you know or what you think you know. Write all that down.

Visit your vision often. It will keep you focused. And if a change is needed, you'll see it in your vision as well.

Sound Play

For extra support as you work with the visioning meditation below, you can tune in to the brow chakra. The sound associated with this chakra is "eye," as we've used before. This chakra is the energy center where we can see our highest vision.

Use this sustained sound of "eye" and feel the color indigo. Feel the vibrations in this area and any other places in your body that you feel them.

Share in your journal about the sensations you felt before, during, and after the meditation and the toning.

Playing in Business

The brow chakra is aligned with your vision. When you're starting and growing a new business or expanding your current business, your vision is the focus and driving image that keeps you on track. This image allows you to answer questions such as *Should I go in this direction?*, *Should I hire this coach?*, and *Should I learn this technique?* It keeps us from chasing after every shiny object that appears on our path.

When you make the "eye" sound, it helps you vibrate this energy center. So play with it when you're choosing your next steps for your healing business. And go through the above exercises to allow yourself to be guided. Let the vision come in clearly so you know exactly what steps are next for you.

This is where you can discover whether you're meant to be doing this alone or with a partner or coach(es). You can see what trainings you may need or if it's time to hire someone to assist you in your business.

If you already did the visioning exercise above, then look into how it can be of service to you and your business. Can you see where you're headed? Read on to learn more about how to use this vision for getting answers along the way.

2. How Can the Voice Help with Visioning?

Do you have trouble getting into a meditative state? Do you find that when you do, it's hard to receive a vision?

I've had clients with both of these situations. One thing that helps them is to use their voice to go into a meditative state. And when I gave them permission to have a vision that isn't "visual," it seemed to help those who couldn't "see" their vision.

Let's start with permission. You have full permission to "see" your vision in any way that works for you. You might see a scene in your mind's eye. Or you might have a sense of it in your body. You may notice other senses giving you information. Take whatever comes to you as part of your vision.

Now for the voice. The Voice Expression practice where you make the sounds for each of the seven chakras is a great way to get into a meditative state. It's not the only way, of course. But if you've had trouble in the past or you want to test it out, feel free. You can find a list of the seven sounds in Appendix A—plus a corresponding video, audio, and full-color chart on my book extras page.

Let's Play!

If it works for you to meditate while you read these instructions, feel free. If you prefer to listen and be guided through this, you can find the audio version of this meditation on my book extras page (URL at end of book).

I invite you to feel the vibrations of each of the sounds you're making. Tune in to that chakra, the color, and the sensations in your mouth, throat, ears, and any other areas where you're feeling sensations. They're all important, so take note.

As you pay attention to each area of your body, you may even feel into your energy field around you. Notice if you sense a different color from the one on the chart.

The important part of this is to be fully present with all the sensations for each tone.

As you complete the Voice Expression practice, you may find that you're in a calm, peaceful state of receiving. Stay in the silence. Feel the vibrations in your body.

When you're ready, while still in this calm state, allow yourself to ask the question of your highest self, God, Spirit, Higher Power, angels, or guides, "What is the highest vision for me in this moment?"

Repeat the question in your head a few times. Give the vision time to form. If it seems fuzzy or unclear, you can imagine moving the veil out of the way or focusing the lens the way you might on a camera. You can zoom in or out to get a better view.

As you see more of your vision, allow yourself to take note of the big picture: Where are you? Are you outside? Or inside? Are you alone? Or are others with you?

Then pay attention to a few details: What are you wearing? What's on your feet? What's on the rest of your body? Is there a hat on your head?

Notice the sounds around you and your other senses: Do you smell or taste anything? Can you touch something and feel the texture? What are you touching, and what is the texture?

Look to your left, your right, above you, below you. Look behind you. What do you notice?

If others are with you, who are they? What are they doing? What are *you* doing?

Ask more questions for clarity so you get every detail of this scene.

When you feel that you've seen and experienced everything there is to see and you're ready to come out of the vision, open your eyes and write down as many details as you can.

If you didn't get details, write down anything that you did get, even if it seems cryptic.

For best results, tell someone about the vision. When we voice the vision in words, we get more clarity, create an ally in the one we share with, and bring our vision toward us in a very powerful way. When my clients share their vision with me, I feel like I'm holding them as they move toward their vision and it moves toward them. I get to be their cheerleader and hand holder, and we can celebrate each step along the path.

Playing in Business

As I mentioned before, your vision is key to guiding you forward in your business. Having this vision accessible helps you make decisions in your business in a way that's easy and focused.

I recommend you tap into this visioning meditation frequently. Write about it, draw it, paint it, share it with others, and keep it fresh in your mind. Think about it when you're alone or with others. Tap into it when you're cooking or doing other daily tasks that are sometimes meditative.

I like to have a snapshot in my mind. For example, mine was me on stage. I didn't need every detail in that picture in order to tap into my vision when making decisions. I just had to pull up that image in my mind and see whether this decision would move me in that direction or away from that image.

We tend to forget our vision when we bump up against something that causes us fear or anxiety, yet those emotions can be very important to process. Later in this book, we'll talk more about ways you can use your voice to process those negative emotions (and celebrate the positive ones too) so you can get back on the path to your vision. For now, though, you can know that your goal is to have a business that serves you and your clients. So if something isn't feeling good, there's usually something out of alignment.

You're being empowered to use your voice to grow your business in alignment with your gifts and your genius. And you don't have to do it all on your own.

3. Why Is It Important to Speak Your Vision?

Have you journaled about your vision? Have you shared it with others? Have you talked about it with your accountability partner or anyone else who can really hear you and acknowledge you? Have you spoken about it to an audience?

I encourage you to share your experience. Now is the time to use your voice in a powerful way.

When I led toning circles, we would pause and sit in the silence, feeling the sounds and vibrations reverberating in our bodies, around the circle, and out to the world. Many people didn't want to break that silence. But when they did speak, the words expressing this shared experience were soothing and affirming for others. The words gave context to what we were all doing together. The words grounded our etheric experience into our bodies and into the earth so we could have a way to talk about it with others.

Words have vibrations of their own. I understand how challenging it can be to put words to an experience that seems to transcend words. Yet when we speak about our experience, we bring that experience into being, into reality.

As we open and activate our throat chakra through the Voice Expression practice, we find our way to expressing ourselves with more ease, power, and grace.

Let's Play!

Continue this Voice Expression practice daily, and it will serve you in many ways. As you read and try the exercises in this book, you'll go deeper into this practice.

I invite you to bring this new power of your voice out to the world. Begin to share your message with the world, even if you don't know exactly what your message is. It's in the speaking that your message will become more defined. So start speaking.

Speak on stage. Speak on video. Speak through writing. Your voice needs to be heard. And your ideal clients need to hear you. They need to hear about your experience, your story, what has helped you. And in that, they'll feel a connection to their own experiences, their stories, and how you can help them.

Use the power of your voice. Go on. I'll hold your hand. You can do it. If you're not quite ready yet, keep reading and doing the exercises in the book. At some point you will be ready. And I'll be here to support you.

Playing in Business

When we show up on video, in writing, or on stage, that's how our clients will find us. If we stay hidden, then our gifts can't reach those who need them. The people we're here to help will never be able to find us.

How would that feel? You came here for a reason. Let the world know what you can do.

As we find our voice, our message begins to be clarified. And as we clarify our message, it becomes easier to share it. It all starts with you feeling empowered with your voice and getting in touch with your highest vision.

When I was making those "weird sounds" that I didn't understand, I heard people say I was going to be helping others with my voice. But I didn't see how. I just kept hearing the message to "just do it." Just make the sounds. Just feel the vibrations. Just begin to share about it. And as I did share in safe communities, I started to discover how I was helping people with my "weird sounds." This helped me step out more and more. I've even stepped out enough to write this book.

So, if I can go from making "weird sounds" and not knowing what to do with them to writing a book about voice and vision, then you can explore the power of your voice too. See what wants to be expressed through your voice. Share with someone. You may discover it gets easier as you go forward.

I recently heard a quote by Tim Elmore: "You can't steer a parked car." So take action in the direction of your vision and express yourself. Your clients will find you, and you'll get closer to living your vision. I'd love to be able to say "I knew you when."

4. How Do Voice and Vision Work Together?

What have you noticed about the power of your voice? Have you noticed its clarity? Its power? Its effect on your vision? What else have you noticed?

As I continued my Voice Expression practice, I noticed more and more parts of my vision appearing in my life. And I noticed that my vision got clearer and clearer every time I tapped into it.

When I first started working with clients on this approach, I was so pleased to hear them tell me the effects that the Voice Expression practice had on their vision and their lives. Their vision got clearer and their voice got more powerful. They were able to express their vision with a strength that I didn't hear at the beginning.

Some clients discovered a vision they didn't expect, which is what happened to Kerry. While working on her coaching business, she rediscovered her love of playing the violin. In her vision, however, she saw herself playing the cello. That soon became her reality: she bought a cello and began playing it. And then she saw herself teaching her daughter how to play the violin. She made this vision real as well, teaching her daughter and other students, first in private lessons and then in classes at her daughter's school.

Another one of my clients, a psychic medium named Gail, used her visioning practice to discover something very unexpected that changed the course of her business in a powerful way. When we started working together, she was struggling to find more clients online. Her vision at the beginning was to spend more time in the fifth dimension. After doing the Voice Expression practice and tapping into her vision regularly together, I noticed she was speaking differently. I felt like she was channeling. In our sessions, we were able to ask questions while she channeled the answers. This channeled entity introduced themselves as the "Soul's Collective" and guided her to her next steps as she changed the focus of her business to include their messages. They helped her set up her new website with marketing copy that was more in alignment with these new gifts, and more clients began finding her with ease. Also, she was reenergized by this new addition to her business and her life.

My client, Cathy, is a gifted healer, but when she came to me, she was having a challenge with making a video to post on social media. We worked with the Voice Expression practice and tapped into her vision—an image of her in a small circle of women whom she supported with her healing gifts. After this experience, she was able to make her video with ease and grace. She posted it and has since made many more videos for social media and for her clients.

But that was just the beginning. The most unexpected piece of our work together came after we'd been regularly tapping into her vision. In one of her sessions, she looked over her shoulder and was startled to see an entire auditorium of people she hadn't noticed before. As we asked questions while she was in her vision, she realized that before then she hadn't been ready to see this larger group. And she realized who they were: not the people she supported directly (women who had their own businesses) but those who benefited from her clients' work. It was exciting for her to see that by helping a small circle of women, her work could touch so many more.

Mary worked with me through the Voice Expression practice and found her way to something she'd had with her all along but hadn't seen. When we met, she was trying to grow her coaching business. She had worked in other businesses and knew the business world well. She had a vision of a building where she could set up her new business and support others with her experience. It just wasn't happening, though. And then she started to turn her attention to her home and her property. She was able to find support via volunteer organizations, and soon she realized that she was enjoying growing crops for her family and her neighbors. She started to see ways she could teach and support others to do the same. Although she'd been a musician and a performer for many years, she said she'd never experienced anything as powerful as using the Voice Expression practice with her visioning work.

Let's Play!

Have you written in your journal about how your voice practice is affecting your vision? Have you shared it with your accountability partner?

Have you been doing the seven-chakra Voice Expression practice regularly? Daily? Weekly? Share about what you're noticing as a result of doing that.

Have you done the Visioning Process? More than once? Remember, the more you tap into your vision, the more you'll be able to bring it into your reality.

If you haven't found an accountability partner to share with, keep writing in your journal. And keep reading for more ideas on how to use your vision to make more profound changes.

Playing in Business

As I mentioned earlier, your business is guided by your vision. Even if the vision you were shown doesn't directly appear to be for your business, stay with it and ask questions about how it can help you.

If your vision is truly your highest calling, there may be subtle or even drastic changes for you to consider in your business. If you're working hard to find more clients, or you feel that having more clients will mean you have to work even harder, tap back into your vision and ask what you need to be shown in order to do God's will with more ease.

As spiritual entrepreneurs, our business may not look like what we see others doing. Maybe you've never seen anyone doing business the way you want to do it. I give you permission to do business *your* way, in alignment with who you're designed to be. The more you align with yourself, the more people will want to work with you.

I've studied with various teachers and coaches to learn different ways to set up an aligned business. Sometimes those people gave me exactly what I needed, and other times I was trying to fit myself into someone else's plan—not Spirit's plan for me.

I also notice that when I feel fear or other negative emotions, I make decisions from a place of trying to figure it out on my own—*my* will. And when I feel the unconditional love of Spirit speaking through my vision and my voice, my heart is open and I feel free to be me.

What do you feel is challenging you the most with your business? What's the one shift that could really support you at this time? Is it having a community around you? Having someone to ground you and guide you through the exact steps to take to get to your vision? Or do you already know the steps and simply need a cheerleader to celebrate you along the way?

Perhaps writing about it or talking with someone will help you to discover what you need support with.

5. How Do You Befriend Your Inner Critic?

Let's check in. Are you finding that you're reading this book and not doing any of the exercises? What is that about for you? If you are doing the exercises, do you feel good about them, or does something inside you keep saying, "You're doing it wrong" or other such things that cause you to doubt yourself?

Read on. I wrote this for you...

Do you have a voice in your head that's always criticizing you? Me too. Mine usually sounds like either my mom or my dad. Often, I'm not even aware that it's talking to me. Does that happen to you?

Or maybe you find that your inner critic can sometimes be worse (and often *louder*) than anyone you've ever actually heard criticizing you. It might tell you things that are so terrible you wouldn't even say them to your worst enemy. Have you noticed that?

When this happens, your first instinct might be to try to silence or ignore that voice—to shush it or block it out. But when we want to heal our own voice, it's important to first befriend our inner critic. How do we do that? Read on to find out.

Let's Play!

When I notice my inner critic, the first thing I do is ask, "Whose voice is that?" Once I identify that, I look at why they're criticizing. Are they afraid? Are they feeling out of control? Are they angry or upset that their needs aren't being met? Do they need attention? Do they need to be heard?

Sometimes the critic I notice in my head turns out to be my inner child. She may be upset that I'm not paying attention to her, so she tries to sabotage my efforts. When I can be quiet long enough to identify the voice of my inner child, I can turn my attention to her. I can sit with her and listen to what she needs to tell me. I do this in meditation or in journaling. Sometimes I like using nondominant-hand writing. I ask the question with my dominant hand and answer with my nondominant hand.

Once I've allowed my inner child to speak to me and I've acknowledged her, then we can come to some kind of agreement to help her feel safe. And she can be busy with something she likes to do while I do this voice healing work I feel I need right now.

Have you connected to your inner child lately? What does your inner child have to say to you?

It's quite easy to befriend my inner critic when I identify it as my inner child. Often, even when I initially think it's my father or my mother or a teacher's voice that's criticizing, as I sit, I may notice that it's actually my inner child hiding behind memories of those authority figures.

If it does turn out to be one of those authoritative voices, I can sit with them as well. I can ask what they're actually trying to say to me as I listen to the echoes of memories of when they said something like that in the past. I can go back to those memories and play with a technique for rewriting our worst memories. To do this, I start by asking myself, "What if that experience actually went like this…?" Then I rewrite this newly imagined, more empowered version of the memory. Next, I ask, "Who would I be if the story went this way instead?" I describe a scenario and an outcome that makes me smile and feel good about myself. This technique lifts the heaviness from the original memory and frees me to be more playful.

If you feel weighed down by heavy memories, you may wish to try this technique as well. You may even find that it transforms inner critics into inner cheerleaders! Are you open to this possibility? What if in the rewriting of the memory, an initially critical person became our advocate who supported our work? What would they say now if it all went that way? Would they be cheering you on now? How does that feel?

You can continue with any other critic voices you hear, each time they come up. It doesn't have to take very long. And it doesn't have to be heavy or hard. In befriending our critic around our voice, it's so important to have a lightness of spirit in our approach. Keep it simple and fun!

Playing in Business

Do you ever have doubts about your business? Me too. Do those doubts stop you from charging what you're worth? Or doing the things that could generate income and helping the people you're here to help?

Do you ever feel stuck, frozen, or overwhelmed? Me too. What helps you get out of that state? Perhaps it would help to try the above exercises to move you through the obstacles that are stopping you from moving forward with your business goals and having your vision come to reality.

If you've been hesitant to do the Voice Expression practice, share about that with your accountability partner. What's coming up around speaking, writing, expressing yourself through your voice or other means? When you can move through the doubts and overwhelm, you can shine your light brightly and allow others to see you.

As one of my mentors often says, "Your clients are looking for you. Not just someone *like* you. They are looking for YOU." So try these techniques of befriending your critic and keep reading and trying these voice and vision exercises. You'll begin to see and feel a difference in yourself and in your healing business.

PART TWO: Wading in a Little Deeper

III. Exploring More Chakra Sounds: The 12-Chakra System

1. Breathing Techniques for Greater Capacity

Breathing in.

Breathing out.

It's all so simple until we start to direct our breath.

While tuning in to your breath and noticing the inhale and the exhale, you may notice a natural expansion of each inhale. So, to create a fuller inhale, allow the breath to expand just a bit more fully.

I invite you to breathe in through your nose at first. Then, after you've filled up with the nasal inhale, you can inhale a bit more by inhaling through the mouth. This beautifully prepares your throat for creating sound.

Staying mindful of your breath during your Voice Expression practice will serve you well.

When I'm relaxed, seated (or lying on my back), I can get a nice rhythm of inhaling, toning, inhaling, toning, inhaling, toning. For me, that creates such a beautiful ease in my practice. Not a lot of effort. It all feels like breathing. The toning is the exhale.

When I'm walking, I notice I need to take extra breaths. This may also be your experience at the beginning of your Voice Expression practice, even when you're seated. Everyone is different. If you find you need extra breaths, notice that. And allow the practice to get easier over time. As you feel more relaxed, you may notice you're breathing more easily.

If going through all twelve tones each time feels like too much, then I invite you to start with one tone at a time. Or maybe just humming. Allow the one sound to be your daily Voice Expression practice.

When you're ready, you can add a second tone and then gradually move to three tones. Maybe change the tone each day until you have a familiarity with each one. Then follow your intuition to choose the next one to add to the single tone. This is *your* practice. Let it serve you.

The most important thing in breathing is relaxation. If you feel any tension while making sounds with your voice, remember to come back to the breath.

Let's Play!

Alternate Nostril Breathing

I learned about alternate nostril breathing in my yoga class with one of my favorite teachers. We did this practice at the beginning of each class, and it was transformative for me.

Even after many years of swimming and singing, I still found myself feeling tension in my shoulders and neck when I was retaining the breath. This alternate nostril breathing calmed this for me.

The basic idea is that you inhale through one nostril and exhale through the other nostril.

We start by using the right hand. Fold your index and middle fingers in toward the palm. Then place your thumb and ring finger on either side of your nose. The thumb will gently close the right nostril and the ring finger will close the left nostril.

The basic pattern is this:

Inhale through the left side, closing the right nostril.

Then close the left nostril, open the right, and exhale out the right side.

Continue with an inhale through that same right nostril. Then close the right nostril, open the left, and exhale left.

So it's inhale left, exhale right, inhale right, exhale left.

Repeat this pattern, counting to five for each inhale and five for each exhale. Try five to ten repetitions. And remember to gently close the nostril each time—don't pinch or squeeze.

Next, add a retention of the breath.

After the inhale, close both nostrils and retain for a count of five before exhaling. After the exhale, again, close both nostrils and retain for a count of five. Repeat this pattern again for five to ten repetitions.

You may choose to add the retentions on your next practice session. Give yourself time to play with these techniques. Maybe do the first one for a few days or a week. Then, after you're comfortable with the simple alternate nostril breathing, add the retention.

You can try different counts. Inhale for four, retain for four, exhale for four, retain for four. (This is similar to the box breathing we did earlier.) Or you can inhale for four, retain for eight, exhale for sixteen, then repeat.

There are many variations, some of which you can find on the book extras page (URL at end of book).

Breath Retention After the Voice Expression Practice

You may want to conclude your Voice Expression practice with this breathing exercise: Start with a full, deep inhale. Retain the breath. Then, as you're retaining that breath, draw up at the perineum and the navel, then lower the chin to the chest. Release the physical drawing-in actions before allowing the breath to return, then resume natural breathing.

These three areas (perineum, navel, chin) are known as the three bandhas—gates or locks you can use to stop and restart the flow of energy as well as breath in the body. I hope you'll try this powerful practice.

After you do, share in your journal which of these breathing techniques you're trying. Which ones will you be continuing? Were any of them confusing or challenging?

2. How I Found My New Voice... and How You Can Too

When I found my new voice, I was very surprised by what I discovered. I didn't know I had such a big voice in me; it had been held back for so long. And I definitely didn't know I could channel anything.

I discovered I can channel light languages and other sounds from many different beings, such as a Cherokee medicine man, Tibetan monks, Mongolian nuns, angels, astral beings, and Hathors (manifestations of the Egyptian goddess). I've even felt whales and dolphins come through. And there are sounds I haven't identified yet. Sometimes the sounds come together, so it's hard to figure out where they're coming from. But I've come to realize that I don't need to know who or what they are. I know they're of the light and for the highest good for all who hear and feel them, myself included.

How about you? Have you found a new voice within yourself? Do you feel something emerging already from the first part of this book? Are you ready to discover your new voice now? What do you want to be able to do or say with this new voice? Or are you just curious?

As I've mentioned before, my client Gail discovered a collective of angelic energy that she now channels through her voice. It began when we were working on her vision after doing the Voice Expression practice together. When she spoke to me from her vision, I noticed how different her voice was. I felt that she was channeling. So I allowed her to speak. I asked questions, and the answers were from a different being than my client. When we completed the initial visioning exercise, I asked her if she knew that she was channeling. She did. But she didn't know who or what she was channeling. So we spent a few sessions getting to know this collective as they answered our questions. Gail was aware and could hear all that was being said. We were both very excited by this new voice she'd found.

A new voice doesn't always come as a channel, however. Although I speak with lots of people who channel, I work with healers in different ways. We often work on the practical aspects of building a business. My client Abby found her voice by making videos. She discovered the strength within her by using the Voice Expression practice, and with coaching from me she gained her confidence to start posting her videos in her Facebook group. Once she practiced making videos, she got over her nervousness and her need to be perfect and found her voice in speaking from her heart on topics she knows will help her clients.

Our "voice" doesn't always have to come from our mouth. For instance, we can speak through a musical instrument. As I mentioned earlier, my client Kerry has something to share with the world through the violin. She found her voice through her playing and also in teaching children how to play the violin.

It's sometimes a challenge to go from musician to music teacher. We doubt our abilities to pass on our understanding of music and our instrument. It can seem daunting to begin to teach all that we know. Where do we start? For Kerry, it started with doing the Voice Expression practice regularly.

Are you ready to explore your own voice? What new voice will you find? I'm excited to hear.

Let's Play!

Journal Play

Explore in your journal:

- What does it mean to you to find your new voice?
- Have you begun to explore the sounds with your voice?
- What are you starting to notice?
- Do you notice that your "new voice" shows up in your business or other areas of your life?
- When you make sounds, what do you feel in your throat? In the rest of your body? In your emotions?
- If you haven't started making sounds yet, what seems to be stopping you? Can you identify those feelings? Express them in writing? What are you needing or wanting more of?

Sound Play

The last time we explored the sound of our crown chakra ("ee"), you were invited to make the sound with others. Now I invite you to explore on your own.

Standing or sitting with your back straight, tune in to the top of your head.

Form the vowel sound "ee" (as in the word *free*) and imagine it vibrating the top of your head, the crown chakra.

Feel the sensations, call in the color violet, allow the energy to flow in from above and down through your being into the earth. You can also draw energy up from the earth through your central column and out through the crown. You can cycle the energy up and down as much as you'd like at whatever speed feels right to you.

When you feel ready, you can begin to explore further:

Calling on the Divine with this "ee" sound, allow the pitch of your voice to rise up a little bit and feel these new sensations. You can continue to float up in pitch and even allow the sound to slide up and down the tiniest bit. Allow this to be playful. Noodle around.

When I do this, I feel like I'm playing with the angelic tones. As you float up there with your voice, you too may feel a beautiful connection with the Divine.

Remember to breathe as often as you'd like, allowing the sounds to be relaxed and easy. No need to push. As you relax, feel the openings in your crown and in your throat. Feel the sound opening the back of your throat and vibrating up in your skull. Feel the smile that comes over your face as you sense the vibrations and the connections with the Divine and angelic energies.

Share in your journal and with your accountability partner about your experiences with playing in the crown chakra and the higher tones.

Playing in Business

You may feel that the support and unconditional love of the Divine through the crown chakra can soothe you as you practice the tools and strategies of building a business.

As we discussed before, the crown chakra is related to our business practices as well as our spiritual practices, which can also be what we need to practice and get better at in our business.

So, after making the sounds above, take a look at aspects of your business. (If you'd like, you can refer to the "7 Proven Steps to Grow Your Healing Business Online" chart in Appendix C.) Is there something you need to start doing more of or that you'd like to be better at? Making videos? Giving talks or workshops? Speaking/writing about what you do and how you help people? Getting clear on who your ideal client is and where you're showing up online? Creating and sharing a program that you'd like to offer?

I recommend choosing one of these ideas—or any other one that calls to you right now—and spending some time deciding how you could get better at that. What's one step you could take in that direction? Is there someone who could help you with that aspect of your business?

Feel the support of the unconditional love of the Divine coming to you as you step forward to practice the areas of your business that may really make a difference for you and for those you'll be helping.

3. Where Is the Balance for My Voice?

Have you ever been told you talk too much? Or that you're too loud?

Or have you had the opposite experience: too quiet? Hardly ever talk?

Do you often feel unclear about what you want to say, so you say nothing?

Or do you blurt out whatever's on your mind?

All of the above are examples of being out of balance with your voice. But never fear, there are things you can do to bring balance to your voice. The throat chakra may be in need of some attention. And believe it or not, we can balance our voice in either direction with the same action: making sound with our voice.

I've been on both sides of this out-of-balance experience. When I was younger, I was usually quiet and shy. I was afraid to speak up at home or in school. But with my friends, I would boss them around and say whatever I felt like. Then, in high school, I started out shy, but when I found a group of friends who made me feel safe and comfortable, I laughed out loud easily, said whatever I felt like, and felt accepted no matter how I showed up.

So maybe you're like me and you have both of these experiences at different times—like a pendulum swinging from one extreme to the other.

Finding balance in your voice doesn't mean you'll lose your personal expression. It means that when you choose to express yourself, you'll trust in your ability to speak clearly and will be more likely to be heard. It also means you can choose to be quiet at times.

Are there times in your life when you'd like to be clearer with how you express yourself? Are there times when you regret saying something?

Let's Play!

Journal Play

I invite you to take a few moments to journal about your experience with your speaking voice.

- Does it seem that you're too quiet? Or too loud?
- In what situations do you notice either or both of those?
- Is it part of your nature?
- Do you wish you were more on one side or the other?
- What would it be like to have balance in your speaking voice?
- How would it feel to have clarity when you speak?

Energy Movement Play

These playful movements can help if you're worried about expressing yourself—such as if you feel an urgency to shout or tell someone off—or they can simply be used to soothe your throat anytime.

Clear stuck or negative energy that gets stuck at the back of the neck by cupping your hands and alternately scooping and brushing away any of that energy from the back of your neck. Just keep brushing gently away, shaking your hands after clearing, until you feel that your neck is clear.

Gently place your hands on the front and back of your throat. (If this is uncomfortable, you can place your hands a few inches away and have a similar effect.) Hold your hands there for about three minutes and breathe. Nothing to do but breathe and feel any sensations that arise. Maybe you'll notice some muscles relaxing, but it's also fine if you feel nothing.

Sound Play

Using the sound of the throat chakra ("ay"—as in *play*), notice how it feels in your throat as you vibrate the sound.

- What do you feel?
- Is it easy? Or does it take effort?
- Is it loud? Or quiet?
- Does it have a harshness? Or is it smooth and soothing?

There's no judgment in this awareness. Notice what you notice without making it right or wrong.

As you repeat the sound of "ay," does it shift?

Make notes in your journal each time you do this practice. Take notice in your life as well. Do you seem more at ease in conversations with others? What about challenging conversations? Are those easier as well?

It's okay if you don't notice any changes. Give it time and consistent playing with the Voice Expression practice as well as focused vibrating of the throat chakra sound.

Playing in Business

In our business we use our voice in various ways: promotion via written words in emails and social media, speaking on video and on stage, and in our programs and healing work.

When we can be authentic in our communications, more people will read and listen to what we say, and it will resonate with many more people. This comes easily when there's balance in our throat chakra.

As an example, being too loud or pushy when we make an offer can have the opposite effect from what we're hoping for. And being too quiet and fearful of speaking can also stop us and therefore not attract our ideal clients.

Regular practice of the Voice Expression practice will assist you with this, as will focused playing with the throat chakra sound of "ay."

Consider making the "ay" sound before recording a video or audio or presenting a talk. See if that helps you feel more confident and comfortable with using your voice. It can also work with writing. Before you sit down to write anything for your business, try making the sound "ay."

After you test out some of these techniques, share about them in your journal or with your accountability partner. Maybe you and they will discover something that really brings things into balance for you.

4. How Much Do I Need to Know About Music?

Do you ever compare your singing to your favorite singer(s)? Why do we do that? Why do we think our voice should be as good as someone who has made it their life purpose and spent many years developing their skills in order to sing as their career?

Have you ever been told things like, "You couldn't carry a tune in a bucket" or "Stand in the back and mouth the words"?

These experiences can make us very self-conscious about our singing voice. We may apply these messages to speaking as well. They may even lead to physical conditions such as sore throats, vocal nodules, or other issues with the neck and throat area. In some cases, these negative messages can be so devastating that we stop making sound with our voice altogether.

But regardless of what you've been told or what you've experienced in this area, I'm here to tell you that it is possible to heal from negative beliefs about your voice.

Let's talk about music for a minute—singing songs, to be specific. Songs have a lot of elements to them: words, pitches (tones/notes), rhythms, harmonies, and more. And if one element is challenging for us, we may not know which element it is if we're not trained musicians. So we may give up and decide we can't sing.

There's also the aspect of others who have said things to us. Many people might say things to us about our singing—family members, teachers, friends, enemies, and more—even if they're completely unqualified to make judgments about your ability to sing. I've even had trained choir directors tell me things about my voice that just weren't true. But I believed that they knew more than me, so what they told me must be true.

Unfortunately, many of the people telling us about our singing voice are older, smarter, in positions of authority, and possibly even feared by us, so we immediately believe what they tell us. But what if they were wrong?

That's music.

What about sound? Music is made up of sound. But sound is not necessarily music. I can hear the sound of my keys tapping as I type this. That's not music. It's sound.

So let's look at the sound of your voice separate from music. We each have our own unique timbre (the sound's "color"). It's the timbre that makes one person's voice sound different from another's and why you can recognize someone just by the sound of their voice.

There are different ways we can make sounds with our voice. We can sustain sound on a vowel, such as "aaaaaaahhhhhhh..." or we can hum some consonants (called "voiced consonants"), like "mmmmmmm..." or "rrrrr...." We can also make sounds with our lips and throat with unvoiced consonants, like *t*, *p*, and *k*. Those sounds aren't able to be sustained, which is why they're called "unvoiced."

When we break down sound into these elements, can you see how complicated it can get when we add words? So many sounds in every word! Have you ever tried to identify every single sound inside a single word, like *love*? Which parts are voiced and which are unvoiced?

I love geeking out about sound, so I'll save that for another chapter. For now, I mainly wanted you to come to the idea that music is different from sound. Sound in and of itself is not music.

So, let's play around here (if you haven't already started by making sound as you were reading this):

Let's Play!

Journal Play

In your journal, explore the following:

- Do you remember any messages you were told about your voice? What did you hear? What did others say to you?
- How did it feel to hear what others said about your voice?
- Have you ever compared your singing to professional singers? Did it cause you to stop singing because you felt you weren't good enough?

- How would it feel to let go of those old beliefs? Would you feel lighter? Freer? Would you feel more encouraged to do more with your voice?

Share in your own journal. Then, when you feel ready, share with your accountability partner or in your community to see that you may be inspiring others with your experience.

Sound Practice

We can hum on an "mmm" with relaxed lips. Try it out. Can you feel your lips vibrating and tickling? Try humming with a low tone to start with. Then try higher tones. Note in your journal the differences in those sensations.

We can also hum on other consonants, like *v*. Try that one. Feel your top teeth lightly touching your bottom lip. Feel the vibration? The tickle? Again, play with high and low sounds and note the differences.

Now try humming on *z*. Notice how your tongue lightly touches the roof of your mouth behind your top teeth. Do you notice any difference when you vibrate on high or low sounds?

I invite you to play with moving from the *m* to the *v* to the *z*. Play with any order. Notice what it takes to change your mouth to move to the other consonants. Go slowly. Really feel the sensations.

Chakra Connection and Play

The chakra associated with these humming sounds is the "Earth Star" chakra, located beneath the soles of our feet. This chakra is our connection to the crystalline core at the center of the earth. The color here is black. So tune in to the black crystals at the earth's core: black tourmaline, onyx, obsidian, labradorite, etc. You can imagine the crystalline core as an illuminated cavern. Many crystals are there. You may see lots of different colors. Tune in to the black ones.

As you make the sounds and tune in to these black crystals, you can imagine an energetic connection from your physical body to the center of the earth. This "grounding cord" can be any diameter but I encourage you to play with a connection the width of your hips, so you can feel the release of anything dark, heavy, or old. Allow whatever is no longer serving you to fall down your grounding cord to be dissolved by these beautiful black crystals with ease. Let go of anything you're ready to release. Perhaps you can let go of some of the old beliefs you identified in your journal writing above.

The buzzing and vibrating of the humming of the *m*, the *v*, and the *z* will assist with dissolving what you're letting go of. (Side note: there is evidence that this type of humming can activate your vagus nerve, which can help calm your nervous system.)

Make notes in your journal. How did you feel when you used these humming sounds to connect to the center of the earth? And how do you feel now that you've released things you no longer need to carry around with you?

For more playful explorations with voiced and unvoiced sounds, check out the "Can We Make Sound with Consonants?" chapter.

Playing in Business

In your business as a healer, it's important to clear away and dissolve old patterns, limiting beliefs, and stuck energies that can get in your way. Sometimes they're ours from our past, and sometimes they've come from others. No matter where they came from, we don't need extra weight, so regular clearing is important.

Using the humming sounds of "mmm," "vvvv," and "zzz" is not only soothing as it vibrates and dissolves the heavy, dark, and old stuck energies, but it can also vitalize us as we draw that energy from the crystalline core up into our being. We're tapping into the power source of the earth and powering up our own energy system as we do this.

I love starting my day with these sounds. I begin my Voice Expression practice each day at the Earth Star chakra, which immediately helps me clear and energize my entire body and energy system. Then I continue up through all the other eleven chakras in the twelve-chakra system—a powerful practice to do daily.

Have you been playing with these sounds on a regular basis? Whether you're making a single sound each day or all twelve, making sound is the best way to empower yourself to speak with confidence about what you do in a way that your ideal clients can really hear you and understand why they need to work with you.

Keep sharing by writing in your journal or talking with your accountability partner. Sharing and connecting with someone helps us get out of our own way.

5. Sounds Without Words? Why?

Have you ever been in a situation where you didn't know what to say? You wanted to respond but couldn't find the words?

I find that at times I don't say anything because I'm not sure what to say. I don't have the words. I often don't think fast enough to respond to someone, and when I do, I don't have all the words I need to make my point clear—especially if it's political or something I have an opinion on but don't have all the research to back it up. It harks back to beliefs formed at my family dinner table: *I'm not quick enough. I don't have a good argument with backed-up research to prove myself.* Now that I think of it, our family dinner-table discussions were a bit like being on the stand in a courtroom. My dad would have made a great lawyer.

In everyday life these days, I don't have to say much. But clearly if I'm writing a book, I have a lot of words in me. And lots of stories to tell. With writing, I have time to put the words together and then go back and edit them. However, when I'm on live video, I need to have an idea of what I'm going to say. I may even practice parts of it, and then I have to trust that the words will come out the way I intend them to.

When I was beginning my own Voice Expression practice on a daily basis, I noticed how freeing it was to make sound with my voice and feel the healing vibrations without the concern about the words.

For many years when I was teaching singing, the words were a very big part of how a song sounded. Often the singer could be singing the right note, but the words needed to be adjusted to get the sound to come out a bit better. It seemed that I was working with singers' words more than anything else.

As I contemplated this aspect of words, I realized that words can get in the way of our singing voice as well as our speaking voice. We think we need to have words to express ourselves.

As I work with clients more and more, using tones without words, we all find the power of sound even more powerful. I'm not saying that words aren't powerful. They have different powers, and when we put them together, there are layers of beauty and expression. But the power of taking them separately is also important to pay attention to.

I've experienced a time when I was making pure sounds with no words, and my energy worker and I both started to hear words in those sounds. I was chanting "I am" in slow motion. It was so slow it was hard to identify at first. "Aaaahhhhh…eeee…aaaa…mmmmm." Then I sped it up a little bit at a time, and gradually we could hear it: "I am…I am." I was then guided to add in a third word: for example, "I am love." What an amazing exercise to see all the aspects of *I am* to identify who I feel I am.

Let's Play!

Journal Play

In your journal, I invite you to write about any times when you felt that words got in the way of you speaking what was in your heart.

- How did that feel?
- What did you do about it?
- What about your childhood? Was there a time when you were criticized about your speaking? Or other situations that caused you to feel safer if you kept quiet?
- Would you like to be able to express yourself more confidently?

Sound Play

Here are some playful ways to explore sound without words:

- Hum a favorite song or chant or sing with "loo" instead of the words. Tune in to how it feels. Can you feel the message in your body?
- Play with the "I Am" exercise: Chant "I am" in any way that calls to you, using one tone, two tones, or more.
- Fill in the blank and repeat with different versions of who you are: "I am _______________." Keep going until you run out of words. Try it each day and see if new words

come to you. How does this feel? Does it make you laugh? Do tears come to your eyes?

- Play with making sounds with your voice to a favorite poem or even narrating your daily life. "I am writing right now, and then, when I'm done, I'll get a drink of water." Let go of any need to edit yourself. It doesn't have to be poetic or rhyme or make sense at all. What does that feel like?
- Tune in to the brow chakra and make the sound of "eye." As you tune in to this sound's vibrations at this energy center, you can call in the color of indigo and then try some of the above exercises again.

What do you notice after making the sound of the brow chakra ("eye")? Did you notice a difference? Did any words come to you that you weren't able to access before? Did you get a new awareness of the power of words and the power of sound without the words?

Share in your journal about your experience.

Playing in Business

We've worked with the brow chakra before in our visioning work. In your business, it's extremely valuable to tap into your vision often. So I invite you to take this opportunity to tap into your vision again.

Take some time to get quiet and tune in to your breath. As you become more relaxed, tune in to your brow chakra. Make the “eye” sound a few times with long, deep breaths. As you tune in to the sensations of this sound and the color and feeling of this chakra, ask to be shown your highest vision.

Ask any questions you may have about your vision. See what’s different. You can start with the snapshot from before and go from there. Or you can allow anything to be shown to you. Remember that a vision doesn’t have to be visual. It may be a feeling or a knowing. You may hear or smell something. Go with whatever comes. Follow it as you give it more of your attention. Allow what you focus on to expand and become more vivid.

Take as long as you’d like. Your vision will have a message for you. Stay with it and take in every detail. Remember to look all around and even behind you. Notice who’s there. Where are you? What do you hear, see, feel, taste, touch, sense, understand, know? Keep asking questions. If you don’t have any questions, ask to be shown your highest vision. Keep asking.

We’ll be going into your vision a little bit later and receiving information from your future self. For now, stay present with what you’re being shown.

When you feel you’ve seen enough, gently come back to your journal and start writing. Write whatever comes to you. Allow the words to flow and notice what comes out. You may not even know what you were going to write. Allow your hand to write.

Allow this journal writing to continue until you're ready to complete that section. Then you can go back and read what you wrote. And then journal about that experience.

6. Can We Make Sound with Consonants?

Over the years, it seemed like my choir directors were always harping on our diction. Usually, they wanted us to pronounce our consonants more prominently—something that's very helpful in singing and also speaking clearly. So, if you're a public speaker (or wish to use speaking in your business, such as through videos, audio recordings, or in-person sessions), you could improve your voice by paying attention to your consonants.

Consonants are the sounds that surround the vowel sounds. They give structure to the vowels. And that, for the most part, is how we form words—at least in the English language. (Other languages have different sounds, so the words are formed differently.)

Most of the sounds we've made so far have been vowel sounds, with the exception of humming "mmm," "vvv," and "zzz," which are examples of "voiced" consonants. The difference between voiced and unvoiced consonants is that the voiced ones can vibrate on a pitch and they can be sustained, usually like humming. Unvoiced consonants are not able to have a pitch, and they cannot be sustained.

When we separate the vowels from the consonants, we have something new to play with. I call this "mouth play" because it involves more than the throat to make them. There's the tongue (the tip, the middle, and the back), the lips, the teeth and the throat (closing and opening). For this section, I'll guide you to some playful sounds.

Are you ready to play with the sounds of consonants?

Let's Play!

Sound Play

To create these sounds, you have to vibrate the vocal cords. But you may not be able to sustain them. Explore each one and notice the vibration. Do you notice whether you can sustain a tone? Can you make their sounds in a high voice and low voice?

Here are more sustaining consonants as before, but in a different way:

- J
- L
- N
- W
- Y

And here are more voiced consonants that are not sustaining (not included in Voice Expression practice):

- B
- D
- G

Here's an exercise to help you feel the difference between "voiced" and "unvoiced":

We played with this one earlier. *V* is voiced. Can you hum on a *V* sound ("vvvvvvvvv..."')? It may feel like a buzzing sound. Can you feel the tickle of your bottom lip as you vibrate with your top teeth lightly touching it?

The same sound, unvoiced, would be *F*. Notice that your lower lip touches your front top teeth. But this time there is only air passing between your lower lip and your top teeth. No humming, right?

Did you try it? Did you experience that the lower lip and top teeth are in the same position for both, but one is voiced (hummed) and the other is unvoiced (just air, no hum)? The *F* makes a sound, but you can't add a pitch or tone to it.

Now play with:

- Z and S
- B and M
- D and N

Which ones are voiced? Which ones are unvoiced?

Now let's play with these unvoiced consonants a little more:

Play with repeating the sound quickly in succession for the ones that can't be sustained (e.g., "b-b-b-b-b-b-b-b"). What is that like? Does it take you back to childhood? Or, if you are a parent, do you remember watching your baby play with these sounds? Notice what parts of your mouth are needed to make these sounds. Where is your tongue? Does it touch the roof of your mouth? Or the teeth?

The following consonants are unvoiced consonants:

- C/K
- F
- H
- P
- Q
- S
- T
- X (K+S)
- Ch
- Sh
- Th

These sounds do not vibrate the voice. You can't sustain them or give them a high or low pitch. Play with repeating these sounds. Use your breath to make them louder or softer. What does it take to repeat the sound (e.g., "t-t-t-t-t-t")? Do you notice your belly having to work? Where is your tongue when you make each sound? Does it touch the roof of your mouth? Your teeth? Is it in the back of your tongue? Does air escape out of your mouth? Between your teeth?

Journal Play

Spend some time writing in your journal about this experience. Have you learned about consonants in this way before? Have you worked on your diction? Are you a speaker? Have you been wanting to be able to speak more clearly?

Playing in Business

As you pay attention to the breath and to the shape of your mouth and tongue, these nuances will serve you as you use sound in meditation, healing, and business. As you enhance your voice for expressing your words from stage or on a microphone, the consonants are the vehicle for creating clarity and structure of your words. You may even start to notice the sounds of other people's words. Do they overpronounce consonants? Or do they drop some consonants, making it hard to understand them? What do you notice? After you've noticed this in others, notice what you do with your sounds in speaking.

Consonants give structure to the sounds, creating words. This reminds me of the root chakra. As you connect with consonants, you may want to connect with your root and the sound "uh." Then maybe add a consonant ("buh, buh, buh" or "duh, duh, duh"). Try various consonants and notice how it feels when they're added to the sound of the root chakra. Does it ground you? I know for myself, I sometimes get lifted up so high with the sounds that coming back to my root feels comforting. Maybe this is true for you. Test it out.

You can write about these awarenesses in your journal. Consider how you can use this information and experience in your business—perhaps for speaking on video, on a podcast, or on stage. What have you seen yourself doing in your visioning? Is public speaking one of the areas you've wanted to be more confident with? How could you practice more?

Share with your accountability partner about this experience and how you're planning to use it in your business and other ways in your life. I'm curious where that discussion will lead.

7. Do I Need to Know What Pitch I'm Singing?

Have you ever been told you're out of tune? Or that you're flat or sharp? Or that you can't match pitch?

I've been told all those things. And I grew up singing and playing piano, so I understand what they mean, but I still didn't understand what that person meant by those words because telling a person they're flat doesn't necessarily help them to fix it. If they know what it means, they are more likely to be able to make the correction. So, let's unpack this a bit.

First, let's go over some terminology:

- *Pitch* – the high or low frequency of a note. High being like that of Mickey Mouse's voice. Low like the growl of a big grizzly bear. In Western music, we label pitches using the first seven letters of the alphabet.
- *Note* – the name of the pitch (e.g., C or G) and the written symbol that represents that pitch.
- *Tone* – the quality of a sound or note.
- *In tune* – when someone is singing in tune, that means they're singing the "right" note—that they're "matching the pitch" of whatever is played, what the composer intended, or what is appropriate for that moment in a song.

- *Flat* – a pitch that's slightly lowered, either on purpose (e.g., B flat is a pitch) or not (a note that's lower than the desired pitch).
- *Sharp* – a pitch that's raised. As with flat notes, there are notes that are sharp on purpose (e.g., F sharp) as well as those that are higher than desired.
- *Match pitch* – when someone plays or sings a note and you make that same sound, your pitch matches theirs. In other words, they are the same.
- *Unison* – when two or more people sing (or play instruments) together and produce the same pitches at the same time.
- *Harmony* – when two or more different pitches produced simultaneously sound pleasing to the ear.
- *Dissonance* – when two or more different pitches produced simultaneously sound unpleasant.

No worries if you haven't grasped all of that. But even if you have, consider that sometimes a person hears something and makes a comment that may not be true. Perhaps it's simply a judgment (e.g., about what harmony does or doesn't sound pleasing). Perhaps they're mistaken (e.g., thinking a note is sharp or flat when in fact it's perfectly in tune). Or they may not understand the terminology they're using. I'm not trying to point to anyone being uneducated here, just that terminology can get confused in one way or another.

So, if someone said something about your singing that upset you, I invite you to consider the above. And perhaps consider a new evaluation.

You might even consider that it isn't really that important here. This discussion is all for the sake of you feeling better about your voice—to help you come to terms with the fact that you have a beautiful voice, no matter what you were told in your past. And beauty is not necessary for this type of voice work either. So maybe we don't need to make any type of judgment about your voice currently.

However, as you work with your voice in a healing way, you may notice changes in your voice's abilities.

Soon we'll play with pitches. But first, let's do a bit of journaling so you can become aware of those things you've been told and, if you're ready, release them.

Let's Play!

Journal Play

What do you remember being told about your voice? Write those messages in your journal or share them with your accountability partner. Get it all out. Feel what that felt like and describe those feelings as well.

Sound Play

Now let's play with pitches. As you make these sounds, you can have the intention of letting go of old negative messages and writing a new story about your voice.

When you sustain a sound with your voice, you're producing a pitch. Try it now:

Aaaaaaahhhhhh.

That pitch may be high or low. You can play with some high notes…

Aaaaaaahhhhhh (think Mickey Mouse)

…or low notes:

Aaaaaaahhhhhh (think big grizzly bear).

A pitch can be anywhere above, below, or in between. There are lots of pitches. Those seven letters repeat over and over and over again, higher or lower. Try some other pitches (while sticking with one vowel sound here for simplicity).

Aaaaaaahhhhhh…Aaaaaaahhhhhh…Aaaaaaahhhhhh…

Now let's have some more fun with pitch by sliding from low to high and high to low. You can use your hand and draw in the air some curvy hills and valleys. (Think about a roller coaster going up, up, up, up, up…and then down, down, down.)

Try going fast or slow, or slide up and down, making wavy and loop-de-loop patterns. There's no way to do this wrong. Just have fun!

Notice that I didn't give you a letter and tell you to make the sound of that pitch. That would be a challenge unless you have perfect pitch, which is when a person knows exactly what that letter/pitch is when you say the letter, and they can sing it perfectly in tune.

Most people don't have perfect pitch. And people I know who have it sometimes admit that it's a curse. So don't worry about not having it. And don't worry about singing any specific note. We're just playing with the idea of pitch and allowing your voice to explore all kinds of pitches without labeling them.

We'll go into more about specific pitches next when we talk about scales. For now, have fun exploring pitch as much as you'd like. And get to know the terms if that calls to you.

Playing in Business

This idea of learning some terminology and coming to a different understanding of pitch (as well as other musical terms) can be empowering.

In your business, the solar plexus is how you empower yourself. And if pitch is one of those areas where you've been injured in your voice, then healing this part of you will show up powerfully in your business.

When you speak about what you do and what you offer, you can play with speaking with a higher or lower pitch. You can vary the pitch of your voice for emphasis. This is not about singing, but about voice expression. Using the "oh" sound with your voice can do that as well.

So I encourage you to play with the "oh" sound and do the pitch exercise above with "oh." Of course, you can play with each of the chakra vowels too. But I recommend starting with "oh." We'll be playing more with "oo" and the sacral chakra together soon.

Write about this experience of playing with pitch. How does it feel when you consider making a video about your business now? Have you noticed any shifts? Are you having more fun? Is it less frightening to consider? Are you starting to feel clearer about what to say and how to say it? What do you think has helped you make that shift?

Maybe you want to make a video for your community about this or write about what's changing for you because of your work with this book.

8. I Heard That the Root Is the Note C

Have you heard about the notes (pitches) assigned to the chakra system? If you have, is it the one where the root chakra is C? And then the others go up from there: C-D-E-F-G-A-B?

I've seen it written that way in many books and other sources. And I'm so curious about it. Are you wondering about that as well? Why is that? Let's dig into that, shall we?

First, what is a scale?

Here are some definitions:

- *Scale* – Generally, a scale is a sequence of pitches that's used as the system for creating music. These pitches (notes) are put together in a sequential order. In Western music, there are specific scales such as major and minor. However, there are many other music systems outside of Western music with much different organization.
- *Diatonic* – As part of the Western system of music, this scale is made up of seven pitches in a specific order of whole steps and half steps (e.g., the major scale, which follows this pattern: whole-whole-half-whole-whole-whole-half).
- *Western Music* (typically Western European and North American) – For many years, this was the only system written about in music history books. However, there are

many other systems in the world that are now included in history books and specific books dedicated to the study of the great variety of musical systems.

- *African Tribal Music** – Studies of various tribes in Africa have shown that each tribe has its own unique scale. They use this scale to create their instruments (or maybe the instruments determine the scale).
- *Indian Ragas** – These are scales used in the traditional Indian music system. These scales are more intricate than the Western major diatonic scale described above.

*I use these examples of non-Western music to show how different scales can look. I am not intending to leave out any cultures. Please understand that there are many, many more cultures with their own unique musical systems.

I encourage you to do more studies if this is of interest to you. For recommended texts on music theory, please visit my book extras page (URL at end of book).

Given this information, are you wondering (as I am) how we could say that an energy system (the chakras) is aligned with a specific scale for all humans to follow, specifically the Western C major scale?

Perhaps there was a need to choose something with seven pitches that would align with the seven chakras, so someone randomly chose the C major scale. Perhaps the frequencies of our chakras do align with those pitches. I don't know the history of how that came to be. I can see how if you're playing music with others to support the chakra system, you would want to agree on what pitches you might use so you're all in tune with one another. (More on this later.)

But here's the thing: We aren't talking about music here. We aren't putting together an orchestra and performing for an audience. We're talking about unique human beings with their own energy system. You are unique. Your frequencies don't have to conform to any other system.

My theory is that each one of us has our own scale. And our voice is a way to discover our own healing sounds and the scale that represents that system of sounds. In addition, I believe that our scale may change from day to day and moment to moment, just as our energy changes.

Personally, I don't need to know the names of each pitch for my own healing. However, if that is important to you, there are tuners and tuning apps you can use on your smartphone or computer (or separate devices) that will give you that information.

But if you'd like to discover your personal scale, here are some things you can do.

Let's Play!

Sound Play

Spend some time making the sounds with your voice for each chakra. You can use my system of vowels for the seven chakras, as we've already been exploring. Here's the system I use:

- Start on a low tone with the root on the sound "uh" (as in *fun*)
- Continue up to sacral – "oo" (as in *too*)
- Solar Plexus – "oh" (as in *home*)
- Heart – "aw" (as in *tall*)
- Throat – "ay" (as in *may*)
- Brow – "eye" (as in *smile*)
- Crown – "ee" (as in *see*)

(See Appendix A for chart and a link to access related video, audio, and a full-color graphic of this information.)

I recommend starting at the root and moving up the chakras. Tone each of the chakras consistently. Daily is best. Once you have it down to a comfortable place where you feel like you're making the same pitches each time you do it, then you've found your scale.

That said, your scale may change slightly through time. Each day your sounds may be a bit different. I invite you to tune in to the feeling of this. It may tell you something about your energy system for that day. Your energy system will change each day and even throughout the day, and you may notice that your sounds change as well. I know mine do.

Play with the sounds and feel your chakras as you do. If you want to get more scientific, you could use a tuner to check out what the pitch is for each of your chakras and write it down each time you do it. You could track the variations over time. I haven't done this for myself, but I would love to hear if you do it.

I'd also love to hear what you've discovered about your scale.

- How far did you take it?
- Was this helpful in relieving that part of your mind that feared doing it "wrong"?
- What have you learned about your scale?
- Did you check the pitches?

Share in your journal and tell your accountability partner about it.

Playing in Business

Knowing your own personal scale (whether you know exact pitches or just the familiar sound of each chakra) can help you in your business in various ways. You can tune in to that part of your business to help you grow and ease any resistance that may be coming up for you.

Try tuning in to these parts of your business and playing with the sound that aligns with each:

- *Root-Platform-Uh* – This is where you show up, where you're "standing" grounded.
- *Sacral-People-Oo* – This is your ideal client, who needs your gifts.
- *Solar Plexus-Shine-Oh* – This is you shining your light—on video, on stage, in writing, etc.

- *Heart-Service-Aw* – This is how you help others with your healing gifts.
- *Throat-Speak-Ay* – This is how you share what you do and how you can help people.
- *Brow-Vision-Eye* – This is your highest vision for your work in this world.
- *Crown-Practice-Ee* – This is spiritual practice as well as business skill that you practice.

(See Appendix C for the "7 Proven Steps to Grow Your Healing Business Online" checklist to see how you're doing with your business in each of these seven essential areas.)

After playing with the sounds of the parts of your business, what have you discovered?

How has making the sound of each part of your business helped you?

Can you see how doing this practice daily could support you, your work, and those you serve?

Please share—in your journal, with your accountability partner, or with a trusted friend or business buddy. Others may benefit from your insights. And perhaps you'll gain insights from others as well.

9. What Can I Expect to Feel?

Have you ever found yourself enthralled with a certain sensation? Have you ever felt vibrations in your body? Have you ever felt so relaxed and at peace in your physical body that you wanted to just stay there for as long as possible?

Those are my experiences when I'm making sound with my voice. Would you like to feel that too? If you have felt it, you know what I'm talking about. And I'm sure you'll accept my invitation to play in that place of sensation.

When I sang in choirs, the vibrations and sounds of other voices joining with mine brought me so much joy and other positive sensations, which have been described in books such as *The Choral Experience* by Ray Robinson and Allen Winold. I know I'm not alone in having these sensations, even if it's hard to put into words. It's a felt-sense that brings me back again and again.

After years of singing in choruses of all sorts and singing in operas on stage, I discovered another sound experience that felt similar but new. I felt this new vibration even deeper and more profoundly.

I first experienced it when I heard a crystal singing bowl and felt its vibrations throughout my entire body. My voice began to vibrate with the sounds within the sounds. As I mentioned in the introduction, I wanted to play in the waves of sound vibrations the way a dolphin plays in the waves of the ocean. My voice danced and wove its way in and out of all the different sounds. I felt like I could stay in that place forever.

In that place, my voice could make sounds that I couldn't seem to replicate outside of my healing sessions with my energy healer. I stayed in a state of curiosity as I tried to revisit my sound travels, exploring and searching for how I made those sounds.

My energy healer and friends told me I was going to be helping people with my voice. When I didn't know how that would look, I searched for a daily practice that could move me toward that work. I heard a message to *just do it*. So I chose a practice of vibrating my voice along with the seven chakras. Years later, that changed to a twelve-chakra practice, but the focus was the same—just do it. Just vibrate my voice each day. Feel those vibrations.

And then I began sharing them with others, and we vibrated together. When I vibrated those chakra tones, I felt them in my body. And when I connected my sounds with the voices of others, I felt something even deeper and more profound. Connecting to Earth and Above. Connecting to each other in a sense of Oneness with Source.

People shared that this practice took them into a meditative state faster, deeper, and more easily. Others shared how their body felt the vibrations that soothed and eased them into a state of bliss. And they all wanted more.

Let's Play!

Sound Play

Let's revisit a fun sound we've already played with. If it makes you smile and laugh, then you're doing it right. If not, then let go of any concern about whether you're doing it "right" and just play like a kid or a dolphin in the waves.

Let's play with the sound "oo" as in *zoo*.

Begin by sitting tall or standing. Take a few moments to tune in to your breath, as we've done before. On the inhale, say to yourself, "I am breathing in," and on the exhale, say, "I am breathing out." Keep doing that—following the breath with your mind as it comes in through your nostrils and out through your mouth.

Allow your body to begin to settle in as you pay attention to your breath. Understand that we'll be making sound on the exhale.

When you're ready, at the top of your next inhale, begin making the "oo" sound. Sustain that sound until you need another breath, then inhale and, again at the top, exhale the "oo" sound.

You can try different pitches—go up or down each time. You can do a little bit of sliding, but for this exercise, go very slowly on any changes.

As you get comfortable with making the sound, begin to notice where you feel the vibrations. In your throat? In your belly? Do you feel it in your back at all? Can you send the vibrations to other parts of your body?

Play as long as you'd like on the "oo" sound. Remember to relax into the sounds, the vibrations, the breath. And follow the way your voice wants to take you. Let it take you away.

If you want to try this with other people who you're comfortable with, invite them to be free. You don't have to be doing the same thing. The fun happens when you can hear and feel how the sounds play against each other.

Playing in Business

Earlier we discussed how the sacral chakra relates to your people in business—including who your ideal clients are and how you help them with your healing gifts. We spent some time designing your ideal, and I recommended that you talk with potential clients to gain clarity. How was that for you?

Now we can go a bit deeper into your ideal clients and also how money plays into this.

The sacral chakra is your money center. Your clients are also the flow of income to you. How do you feel about the money conversation? Is it easy for you to charge what you're worth? Many healers are challenged by this.

Many of us are so willing to give our gifts freely from our hearts. There are some residual energies around not being able to charge for God-given healing gifts. In previous times, we did our healing without financial compensation. And healers were supported by their community. It's a very different time now. We have to pay for our own living expenses and plan for our future. Money is very different than it was in those days when healers were given a place to live and fed and clothed and cared for in all the necessary ways of life.

We said yes to this assignment on earth at this time. Many of us are awakening to our gifts and realizing that many people need our help. So it's time for us to be seen and well paid for helping others.

Let's consider this as we play with the "oo" sound again. Allow the sound to soothe any old beliefs around not being paid for your healing gifts. Allow the sound vibrations to release those old thoughts and antiquated ways.

As we clear out old ways, we open to the new. How would you like to feel about money? About being paid well for your healing gifts? Can you see it as an energy exchange? You give of yourself, your gifts, your training, and your expertise, and in exchange, your clients give you money.

How does that feel?

When we're clear about who we're attracting and the specific needs/wants they're searching for—and we know we have the ability to fulfill those desires—then the money flows with ease as well.

Take some time with the "oo" sound to call in that ideal client. Ask that client in your mind—and in your heart—to share what they need from you. If it feels in alignment, then you're getting clarity.

Once you know you can help your clients with something specific, then you can begin to share about it out in the world. Where can you share about it?

We'll be talking more about your platform as a place you show up and about the idea of "shine"—where you can show up as your full self. When you show up and offer your solution from your heart, people will stop scrolling on social media and take notice of you. Your ideal clients will lean in, take the action you recommend ("click here," "book a call," "schedule a session," etc.), and pay you to solve their problems.

Share in your journal what comes to you about this ideal client. Then tell your accountability partner or a business friend about it and see if it's clear to them. If not, see if they can help you define your ideal client even more.

I'm so excited for you to gain this clarity for your business clients.

10. How Can I Use My Voice to Heal My Body?

Do you ever feel a strange twinge? Or a pain you haven't had before? Ever feel just a bit off?

Sound can be a beautiful way to discover what our bodies are trying to tell us. I like to start with my Voice Expression practice and tune in to how each chakra is resonating and feeling. I'll notice how my voice feels. What the sound is like. Is it softer than usual or louder than usual? Is it a little raspy or sticky? I notice it without judgment and then notice if there's a shift as I make the tones a few times.

If you try this, go easy. It's not about forcing change but rather about allowing a shift to happen. See if it does. Accept it if it doesn't.

Another way to use sound for specific areas of the body is to tune in to that area and make the sound it wants you to make. Or you can just make any kind of sound, notice it, stay with it, and see if it changes.

If you're in pain, you can give the pain a sound and play with the sound until it relieves the pain. If you stop making the sound, does the pain come back? Test it out. Try altering the pitch of your voice. Try soft sounds or loud sounds. Follow your intuition.

You can also talk to the pain. That's what I did once when I felt pain in my right foot that radiated toward my heel and up my leg. My Voice Expression practice wasn't shifting it and neither were the various stretching and other remedies I tried. So I finally asked the pain what it wanted to tell me. As I tuned in, I could feel the energy of my dad. I remembered that he had struggled with this type of foot pain. What I heard could only have come from him. It seemed very unrelated to my foot and leg. And when I heard it, the pain was gone. The message the pain (and my dad) had for me was, "Write, and the rest will follow."

That message became the motivation and encouragement for me to write this book.

I encourage you to test this out for yourself. What are the sounds saying to you? What does the pain want to tell you?

Let's Play!

Journal + Sound Play

- Write down anything in your body that feels off. Then take the time to work with sound to see how it might shift or if your body is trying to send you a message.
- Write down any of these techniques you've tried so the next time an issue arises, you'll remember what worked for you.

- If you're a healer who helps people with their bodies, I encourage you to try using sound to shift something for your clients. Use your voice or encourage them to use theirs. And be sure to document what works.
- If you try something that doesn't work, try again in a different way next time. Keep playing with various ways to make sound with your voice. And try not to overthink it. Just let the sound come out.
- Play with the "aaawww" sound to tune in to your heart chakra. Ask your heart to guide you to your next steps. It may guide you to another chakra and the sound associated with it, to another part of the body, or to some sound you didn't expect to make—like screaming, crying, or expressing anger.
- After you've tested out some of these practices, whether or not you've felt a shift, please share about your experience with your accountability partner. It really helps to know we're not alone in this world. There's something about pain that, in my experience, can make me feel alone, like there's no one that can help me. But sometimes just expressing that relieves the pain. Maybe you'll experience something similar. Hearing about your accountability partner's experience also might help. I know it helps me to hear from other people's experiences.

Playing in Business

Being able to shift out of something that feels off is powerful healing. Have you done that for yourself before? Or for others?

In our healing business, we're often asked to shift how we do things. One example is something we discussed earlier: shifting from seeing patients one at a time to offering a program. How does that possibility feel to you? Is that something you'd like to offer?

No matter what you offer—single sessions, packages of sessions, or a bigger program—let's use this time to discuss how you're offering your services.

Is it difficult for you to offer your work to people even when you know you can help them? Do you stumble over the words? Do you freeze and later think of what you could have said?

As I've discussed in this book (and in my "7 Proven Steps" program), the heart chakra is associated with service. So, as we explore possibilities for you to serve in your business, let's use the sound of "aw" to soothe your heart. As you do, feel into your heart space and remember that you've been given your healing gifts for a reason. The Divine didn't give you these gifts and then leave you hanging. We've already worked with connecting to the Divine with your crown chakra and your voice. Now let's tune in to your heart.

Feel your connection to your clients. Tune in to what they're needing or wanting in their life right now that you have the solution for. That's exactly how you can speak to them. As you tune in to your heart, tune in to one client at a time (a real or potential one). Feel what they're coming to you for and how you could offer your services to them.

How would that feel? Maybe you'll want to shift something in yourself or in your business. This shifting and healing work, along with the sound of "aaawww" will really assist you with speaking to your clients about how you can help them. Make the sounds and soothe your heart. Trust this process. You definitely have something that people want and need.

Once you've come to a bit of clarity about how you're being of service to your clients, write about it in your journal or share it with your accountability partner. Let them know what you discovered. If you find this challenging, share that as well. We'll go deeper into this later in the book, so keep reading.

11. What About the Colors of the Chakras?

When you close your eyes, do you see color? Do you hear color? Do you see sound? Do you feel color? Or sound?

I don't see color when I close my eyes, but I feel it. I also *know* it. And I see more colors around me when I'm making sound with my voice. I don't just *hear* sound; I feel it and interact with it.

When I'm driving down the road, doing my daily Voice Expression practice, I find myself noticing the color associated with the chakra I'm toning. For example, if I'm toning the root chakra, I notice red things around me. I might notice a fire hydrant, a red car, or red leaves. It's fascinating how many things of that color pop into my view as I make the sounds.

I have a past-life memory of working in the tombs under the Great Pyramid in Egypt where I was walking through the halls with smooth black walls. I entered the throne room as a high priestess. The guards greeted me as I entered and passed through, into my treatment room. The treatment room had a large stone table adorned with crystals and a hanging mobile above with large, flat crystals. A beam of sunlight shone through the ceiling, and the mobile could be adjusted to beam certain colors onto the person lying on the table as I created the sounds and used other healing modalities.

This memory, and the fact that I was guided to this place by a dear friend, is significant because this friend is a color therapist. We've done quite a few projects together where we've combined color and sound, and we're very aligned with what comes through for the greatest healing of the most people. For example, when I tuned in on 12/12 (December 12) to discover the twelve chakra tones, she had also done the same on her own and discovered the twelve colors associated with those chakras. She's also discovered that some of the colors are shifting to new shades, which is exciting as well.

It makes sense that we would combine color and sound. After all, they are both forms of vibration.

This connection with color reminds me of the Soul Star chakra, located about six inches above the head. This chakra is about our higher expression. The color associated with this chakra is magenta, and the sound is "ih," as in the word *kiss*.

I invite you to play with color while you're making sounds with your voice.

Let's Play!

Playing with Colors

Use the chart in Appendix B or visit phoebefazio.com/book-extras to see a full-color chart of the twelve chakras to tune in to each chakra's color as you make the corresponding sound.

- As you make a sound, notice what color you see (or feel, sense or know). Does it match the one on the chart? Or is it something different?
- Close your eyes and feel what color is associated with the sound you're making in that moment.
- With your eyes open, look around and notice the colors that become more vibrant as you make the sounds of each chakra.
- When you make the sound of a specific chakra, imagine yourself wrapped in that color as you tune in to that area of the body and what's coming through or activating for you.

Sound Play

Tuning in to the Soul Star chakra, connect with the color magenta and feel the sensations above your head. Tap into your higher self and make the sound "ih." Sustaining this sound sometimes feels unusual. Let go of this sensation and feel the vibration in your voice and elsewhere in your body.

It may be helpful to feel the sound and the color wrapping around you, as if there were a cocoon or a pod that starts about six inches above your head and comes around your sides and front and back about the same distance away from your body. Feel the light and color magenta as you sustain the "ih" sound.

Stay with that as long as you wish. Then go to your journal and write:

- What did you feel?
- Did you see, feel, or otherwise experience the color magenta? Another color?
- Can you tap into your higher self?
- Is there anything you'd like to ask your higher self?

Share some of what you've written with your accountability partner. I bet they'd love to hear.

Playing in Business

In my "7 Proven Steps" program, I also include the five other chakras in the twelve-chakra system. The Soul Star chakra is a very important part of this. We tap into it for inspiration and guidance.

As in the above journal prompts, you can ask your higher self questions about your business. You can ask for guidance about moving forward.

I often ask my angels to help me with tasks in my business. This might be a good time for you to explore that if you haven't done this before.

The angels are always here with us, ready to help, but we have to ask for help. They can't step in until we ask.

I like to have an angel assistant who gathers teams of angels to help me. Whether it's to write emails, make phone calls, or do anything else in my business that I don't really enjoy, the angels can handle these tasks for me. I really do feel them doing it. It helps me so much.

What would you ask the angels to help you with? They can help with just about anything. So go ahead and ask.

Then, if you'd like to, share in your journal or with your accountability partner how tapping into the Soul Star has been for you. Are you doing the Voice Expression practice yet? If so, share a bit about how that's been for you. What are you noticing?

IV. Using Your Visioning to Go Deeper

1. Supercharge Your Visioning

When I first felt into the twelve-chakra tones, I was especially in love with the cranial chakra, which brought me into a more powerful connection with my brow chakra and visioning. At the time, I hadn't heard anyone talk about this subtle chakra, although I've since seen some information that sounds similar to what I've experienced.

Accessing this chakra vibrated my head in a new way. I could feel the glands in my brain being activated (pineal, pituitary, and hypothalamus). I played with focusing the sound forward toward my brow, which took me to higher dimensions and to a sensation of calm and ease.

When I want to go into a deep visioning meditation, I'll spend some extra time using the sound of this chakra. With this sound vibration, I see more clearly, notice more details, and have access to more of the nuances in my vision.

Over the years of playing with my Voice Expression practice, I've noticed how often this chakra and its sound comes in to support my work in my Reiki sessions. This unique humming sound is often the starting place for overtones (higher pitched sounds that float above the single tone without changing the original pitch) and other sounds in my Sound Washings.

Below, you'll be guided to play with the cranial chakra's sound.

This chakra is located at the back of the skull, where the skull connects to the spine. It is a sensitive area. If you reach back and feel with your fingers, you will feel the arch. Gently move your fingertips around this area until you feel that very sensitive space. Then place your palm gently over this area while you make the humming sound of "ng." (See below for details.)

The sound will vibrate there and radiate forward toward the brow chakra, activating and nourishing the pineal, pituitary, and hypothalamus glands. These glands are necessary for our elevation to our highest selves as we prepare for the New Earth and the changes that have already begun.

Are you ready to explore this unusual chakra and feel more power in your visioning experiences?

Let's Play!

What came to you as you read about the cranial chakra? Any insights?

Are you curious about how to use your voice to activate your pineal, pituitary, and hypothalamus glands?

Sound Play

The sound for the cranial chakra is a humming sound made with the "ng" sound, as in the end of the word *wing*.

Let's make this sound. Begin by tuning in to your breath, as we have for each of the sound practices before. Notice the inhale (mentally say, "breathing in") and the exhale (mentally say, "breathing out").

As you reach the top of an inhale, begin the sustained humming sound of "ng."

Feel the sensations in the back of your tongue as it contacts the soft palate at the back of the roof of your mouth. Try not to think too much or else your tongue may get confused. If that happens, say the word *wing* and sustain the "ng" sound.

Direct the sound vibrations in an arc along the roof of your mouth toward your brow. Can you feel the glands beginning to plump and come to life? (Don't worry if you don't feel it.)

Breathe as you need to and repeat the sound until you feel a natural stopping place (maybe three times or so). Be gentle and easy with this. No need to push. This is a very internal sound and experience. Allow the sound to float.

Enjoy these connections with the magical sound of "ng" and the cranial chakra.

As you complete this sound practice, take a few moments to sit in the silence, feeling whatever you feel.

When you're ready, describe your experience in your journal. And if you feel comfortable, reach out to your accountability partner to share too.

Playing in Business

The power of the cranial chakra for our healing work in the world is a deep and subtle one. As we connect with our spiritual being and our human experience, we can expand our expression in a gentle way that allows us to move through this human experience with grace and ease. We can face our human tasks in our business with the grace that moved us to begin our work in the first place.

I've come to understand that the cranial chakra can activate any other chakra. I usually combine it with the brow chakra since they're linked, moving energy and awareness from the back of the skull forward toward the brow. When combined with the brow and visioning, we can use this activation to help bring that vision into our current reality.

When we take the time to connect with our spiritual self, and with those beautiful beings who are looking for us and needing what we offer, then we're more aligned with our healing work and how it's manifesting in the world around us.

I encourage you to combine this sound practice with your visioning. Before you begin your visioning practice, make the humming "ng" sound. Bring that vibration forward, moving into the brow sound of "eye." Stay with these sounds until you feel complete. Then sit and receive the highest vision that the Divine wishes you to experience (see, hear, feel, know, understand, etc.).

(To access a recorded meditation using these sounds, please visit phoebefazio.com/book-extras.)

After you complete your visioning session, write down what you've received. Notice as many symbols or messages as you can. Write them all down.

- What new insights did you receive for your business?
- Was it the same vision as before? Or different?
- What was different? A new perspective? New details? Ideas? Next steps?

After you've written about this, read on to learn more about what other things you can do with your visioning practice.

2. How to Figure Out Your Next Steps

Have you ever received a vision that was so far in the future that you didn't know how to get there? Have you ever let go of a vision because of this? What about a vision that scared you? Or one that seemed so impossible that you couldn't see your way there?

My clients often tell me they've had these experiences. I have too.

I've come to realize that visioning isn't a one-and-done event. In order to keep a vision alive, we need to revisit it. The more often we do, the more engaged we are with it and the more likely it is to become our reality. So we'll be doing that here in this section.

Here's a trick to finding out how to get yourself to your vision. It's quite simple and when I tell you, you may laugh at how simple it truly is.

1. Go back into your vision.
2. Stand in your vision as if it's the present time.
3. Look back through time from the completed version of your vision.
4. Ask what steps you took to get there.
5. Ask what the first step was that you took.

6. You can repeat this process each time you want to know your next step.
7. You can even have a conversation with your future self in the completed vision, talking to your current self who's just about to take that first step. Your future self can give advice or encouragement as you go.

When I had the vision of myself standing on stage, I looked at what my first step was. I saw that I hired a mentor to guide me toward my vision. Someone who was doing what I saw myself doing and was teaching the exact steps to get there. The images from my mentor's marketing were exactly in alignment with what I saw myself doing. That was confirmation that she was the guide for me. When I hired her, I felt so on purpose with my work. All the pieces came together in a focused way to create the momentum I needed.

This is such a powerful step along the way toward living our vision that we often don't even think of it. So go back to your vision and have fun with what you discover.

Let's Play!

Journal Play

After revisiting your vision, write in your journal the information you discovered.

- What was your first step?
- What steps did you take after that?

Write them down so, as you complete each step, you know what's next.

Can you see the map to get from here to there? Draw it out.

Now go share it with your accountability partner and, if you feel comfortable, with your community. Talk about the steps you saw in this exercise. And then cheer others on as they share about their next steps toward their vision.

Sound Play

It's very powerful to do the Voice Expression practice before diving into your vision. If you don't have much time, at least make the sound "eye" to tap into your brow chakra and support you in visioning. You can tap gently on your third eye, using the color indigo and the lapis lazuli crystal (if you have that available) to support your visioning experience. If you don't have this crystal, use your imagination or an image.

If you'd like to add a second sound, add the "ng" sound of the cranial chakra to activate your visioning experience. Test it out to see how to go from one step to the other. See what feels the most wonderful for you in this moment. In addition, touch the cranial chakra and use the color lilac and a crystal like lepidolite to activate your vision even further.

Spend as much time in your vision as you'd like. Ask your questions and get clear on your next step toward that vision. If you need help taking that step, ask your future self to show you how to get that assistance. Maybe it's by asking the angels. Or maybe it's by hiring a mentor or coach to guide you.

Playing in Business

Having a clear vision for your business is an essential piece of growing a viable business. And having this tool of a clear vision will help guide you there.

Each time you have a decision to make, turn to your vision. Look back at the map you created. It may change slightly, but trust that vision and what you've been guided to do in order to live your vision.

Use the sounds above (plus the color, crystal, and touch) to go deeper into your healing business vision. Feel the power of that vision. Trust that you're being guided every step of the way.

How often will you revisit your vision? I like to revisit mine before I fall asleep at night and then, in the morning, write about it as if it's already happening.

I invite you to write about your vision of a healing business so that you can be there for the clients who are looking for you.

3. How to Move Past Obstacles

Have you ever gotten stuck in a vision? Not sure what to do with it? Feeling some resistance to it? Do you notice feeling afraid?

This happens. And it's often the reason we don't actually get to the place of living our vision.

I've felt that way. And I have a solution for you.

Go back to your vision often. Go to sleep at night with it playing in your mind. Allow the details to be revealed as you drift off into slumber.

Also go back while you're awake. Write down every single detail. There may be some details you can't see for a while. But each time you go back, you'll probably be shown new details.

My vision of being on stage in front of a full house auditorium was so clear. But the one detail I kept asking for and couldn't see was about the content of what I was doing on stage. I could see that I was alone, but I couldn't determine if I was speaking, singing, performing Sound Washing, or facilitating a workshop. That part of the vision didn't appear for years.

So, in the meantime, I focused on the things I did know and continued to go back through the steps I took to get there. I had plenty to focus on without knowing that one thing.

Looking back, I realize that what kept me feeling stuck was that I wanted to know all the details before taking the first step. It was just like when I was told I was going to help people with my voice. I felt I needed to know *how* I was helping people. But what I needed was to take the next step and to pay attention to how it felt.

Focusing on the feeling is the key when we don't have the details.

Let's Play!

Journal Play

I encourage you to trust what you're being shown in your vision. Play with the information and see what it tells you. Which details help you feel the desire to have this vision become your reality?

You might start by making a list of each of those details. It's like when we have a confusing dream, we can look at each symbol and discern its meaning to us. What emotions or associations do your vision's details bring up for you?

After you make the list of details/symbols, write about each one. Don't hold anything back, even if it feels unrelated.

- How does this symbol make you feel?
- What does it remind you of?
- What does it want to communicate to you? Have a dialogue with it.

Sound Play

Use a combination of the "eye" sound of the brow chakra, the "ng" of the cranial chakra, and the "ee" of the crown chakra. These three chakras in combination can be helpful in activating and opening the back of the skull to receive divine guidance to help you see the vision that wants to be expressed through you.

Remember, this is your highest vision being shown to you. You can trust that it's safe for you to see it and express it. If blocks come up and you feel confused, this is usually a bit of fear coming up to protect you. It could be from childhood, or it could be a habit that you've been in.

I'm learning to notice habit emotions that come up for me often. For instance, when I notice fear, I take some time to journal about it or make some sound and hold myself as a loving parent would hold a child. I give myself time and space to feel these feelings. It's safe to feel. And it's important to acknowledge these habits and let them move through us.

If it's not enough to make the sounds of the three chakras above, you may want to go through the entire Voice Expression practice and sit with your vision afterward.

Then share about your experience with going back to your vision for details. What did you discover? What's still confusing?

Playing in Business

Sometimes our vision is so clear that we get a big list of things to do. Other times we struggle to understand what exactly this vision is trying to tell us. Wherever you are with your vision, revisiting it is the way to get answers for your business.

I encourage you to do the exercises above with the focus on your business. You can ask for details regarding your clients and how you're making money.

- Where is the money coming from?
- How will you make a living?
- Who are your people?
- Where will they find you?
- Ask any other questions you have about your business.

If you're not receiving answers from your vision, it may be helpful to talk with someone (perhaps your accountability partner) about your vision and what's challenging you at the moment.

A healing business has different elements from other businesses. We can be triggered in various ways. But knowing that you're not alone on this journey can be a lifesaver. I encourage you to reach out rather than give up.

4. Where to Find the Wisdom

Have you ever looked back on choices you made and, with your current wisdom, see what you would have done differently? What if you had the wisdom of your future self to help you with your current decisions?

You do!

You can use your vision to tap into that future wisdom. You can ask your future self anything while you're in your vision. And the more you get used to that vision, the quicker you can tap into it.

I discovered this technique when I was guiding my clients through the power of their vision. While they were in their vision, I would ask questions and they had the answers because they were actually there. I was able to talk with their future self.

Then I did that for myself in my own vision. I realized how much information is in my vision. I could tap in and get answers. I could find the wisdom in the future to assist me in getting there. I could ask how I got past my current struggles with self-doubt and fear. I could find answers to what kind of support I could turn to for guidance. I could even be guided and encouraged by my future self.

I felt like I'd found a goldmine. And I'm excited to share it with you. Let's test it out. Are you ready?

Let's Play!

Vision Play

What are you struggling with in terms of living your vision? What challenge is coming up for you around actually having your vision become your reality right now?

Just as we've done already, go into your vision now. Really get in there and feel all the yummy details. Experience how it feels to be living that life. Your life. Your future. Stand in this future as if it were your present. You're really there, living that life.

From this vantage point of having arrived at this place, you have wisdom to share with your past/present self. Allow yourself to be both. Ask your future self for the wisdom you need at this moment.

Be willing to receive the answers. Be open to hearing something you hadn't thought about yet. (If you had thought about it, you wouldn't be searching right now.)

Ask how this could be easier. Ask where you could have more support. Ask your future self to share their wisdom with you.

Receive the answers. Feel them in your entire body. And then take action. Do what your future wisdom is guiding you to do. Notice how that feels. Then keep going back into your vision and asking for the wisdom of your future self to guide you.

Next, we'll go into a technique for having regular conversations with your future self. For now, just feel how it is to connect with the wisdom of your future self.

Write in your journal what you've discovered from your future wisdom. Then share with others about your experience with this exercise.

Sound Play

Let's play with the brow chakra sound of "eye" as well as a few supporting sounds—the Soul Star sound "ih" and the Galactic Gateway sound of "rr." (This sound may evolve into overtone singing, which I'll share about later.)

Begin with the "eye" sound of the brow chakra. This can support you as you enter into your vision. Feel the vibration at the third eye as you make the sound of "eye." Imagine the color indigo and any crystals of that color, like lapis lazuli.

Then feel the energy rising above your head to the Soul Star chakra, making the sound "ih." Sense the color magenta and tap into your higher self.

Feel the energy rising up even higher above your head (about an arm's length) and open the Galactic Gateway with the sound "rr." Open the gates with your hands and allow the pure white, effervescent light to beam down through your crown to enlighten your brow and shine light on your vision.

Try combining these sounds in different ways: eye-ih-rr or rr-ih-eye or ih-rr-eye…or any other way that feels fun for you. Feel the buzzing and the connection to your wisdom.

The energy, light, and sound vibrations can nourish and awaken your vision. Allow yourself to use these amazing vibrations to guide you and bring you the wisdom of your future self. Spend as much time as you'd like playing with the sounds.

Then, when you're ready, write down anything you'd like to about that experience with those three sounds, the colors, the crystals, and the wisdom of your vision.

Playing in Business

In our healing business, sometimes our vision is clear and we know what to do to get there. And other times we can find ourselves very confused, resistant, or doubtful that we can even get there. We may even abandon our vision, deciding we don't want it after all.

At those times, it's helpful to have supportive wisdom from our future self who has already arrived at that vision. This can be a lifesaver for your business and all the people you'll be helping with your healing gifts.

Here's a meditation that can help you meet with your future self.

Imagine it's five years in the future. You've gotten your business to a nice place where you're helping lots of people and you've helped many, many more over the years. You have more money now than you ever had, and you feel very happy with the life you've created for yourself.

Notice where you're living. What does the house look like? Is it your current house? What furniture do you see? What else do you notice about this home?

There's a knock at the door. You open the door and see your past self there. You invite them in. You ask them to sit, and you enjoy tea together.

You remember what it was like for you five years ago. You remember the doubts and struggles you were going through at that time.

You have wisdom to share with this past self. What do you say to them? What do you wish you'd heard when you were struggling?

You share freely and answer any of their questions. When they get up to go, you give them a hug and offer some final words of wisdom. They leave feeling grateful for what you shared.

What was the wisdom your future self shared with you? Write about it in your journal.

I did this exercise at a time when my business was still new and I wasn't sure if I was going to see my vision come into reality. I felt so much gratitude for what my future self told me. She was so encouraging and reminded me of the support that's here for me every step of the way.

In that moment, I decided that my future self would be the first person I'd go to for answers in my business. She's already done it, and she can help me with decisions I need to make.

Since then, I've found her guidance extremely valuable. It saves me so much energy and wasted time. Often I would have gone down a dead-end road if I hadn't first checked in with my future self.

What has your future self helped you with today? How often will you check in with this wisdom going forward?

If you feel called, share about your experience in ways I've suggested before—or maybe you'll find another way to share.

5. How to Find the Answers

Now that you've discovered the wisdom from the future, are you ready to have regular conversations with your future self?

I discovered I could use a journaling technique where I could get answers to some of my most pressing questions. This helped me with big life decisions and saved me from hours and hours of worry and uncertainty.

I first learned this technique from a friend who studied with Ira Progoff, a psychotherapist whose intense journaling approach has many techniques. For now, I'll share one simple one that I find very useful for talking with my future self: "nondominant-hand writing."

Here's how it works:

We write down a question for our future self with our dominant hand and then write the answer to that question with our nondominant hand.

I like to use initials for each. You could use "Q" for the question and "A" for the answer. Or use an initial for your name and then "FS" for "Future Self." Or even better, give your future self a name and use that initial.

For example:

P: What am I speaking about on stage in my vision?

T: You're sharing your story of how using your voice helped you to live your vision.

I'm always amazed that the answers come. Sometimes I get the answer as I'm writing the question; other times, I have no idea what my left hand will write...until it starts writing. So fascinating!

Are you ready to try it?

Let's Play!

Have you ever used nondominant-hand writing?

Did you try having a conversation with your future self?

What did you discover from these conversations?

Have you found support from the answers you received?

In Ira Progoff's intense journaling approach, there are unique meditations called "Entrance Meditations." (You can find them at phoebefazio.com/book-extras.)

You can start with one of these meditations and then go from there into the conversations you'd like to have with your future self.

I made these recordings for my friend who taught me some of these techniques. She's now passed on to nonphysical, so use them with her blessings.

I'd love to hear if you used this technique of having conversations with your future self. Feel free to let me know via email.

Sound Play

For connecting to your higher self and to support you on your journey toward bringing your vision to life, I encourage you to play with the sounds of the brow chakra ("eye"), cranial chakra ("ng"), and throat chakra ("ay").

It's fun to start any of the sounds with the cranial sound of "ng"—for example, "ng-ay" or "ng-eye."

You might play with these sounds before you have your conversation, or you may feel called to go back and forth between sounds and writing. Allow the process to unfold for you.

Allow the sounds to support your process of connecting to your future self. You can also call on the colors, crystals, and symbols.

Playing in Business

After meeting your future self in the last chapter, do you want to get to know them even better?

What would it be like to have your future self available to consult with about anything in your business?

Whenever you have a decision to make, ask your future self. See what they have to say to you.

Being able to continue your conversation with your future self can be a huge asset in your business. And having a regular practice of writing this conversation down may provide the guidance you've been craving.

Sometimes, as healers, we work so hard at our business and forget that we can approach our business from the same spiritual practice that guided us to want to pursue these healing gifts in the first place.

I invite you to test this out. See how it goes.

And then write or talk about your conversations.

PART THREE:
Diving in Fully

V. Diving Deeper into Sound

1. Find the Power of Your Breath

I first recognized the true power of breath during labor and the delivery of my first child.

I had learned breathing techniques in childbirth classes. And as a vocal music teacher, I'd taught many people how to breathe correctly for singing. But when I felt the intense pain and fear of contractions before birth, I discovered something I was not prepared for.

Yet, from a wise place deep within me, I found a power to soothe the pain, calm the fear, and release the tension my body felt. I found the strength to continue.

I discovered the depth of my breath. I could inhale into areas of my body where I never imagined the breath could travel. And as I followed the breath into and around all the areas in need, I could feel the breath expand me and bring me healing oxygen—even when my body shook with a desire to push, sensations I was not familiar with, having never given birth before.

My labor was short but extremely intense. It came on fast and furious, so I didn't have time to prepare. I wasn't planning to ask for pain medications, but afterward I wondered when that time would have been. There was no time for that.

Throughout the experience, my mind was unsure. I forgot all that we were taught in those childbirth classes. But with the help and focus of my husband breathing with me, I could focus on my breath. And I could use my breath in deep and powerful ways.

This was before I discovered yoga. Before I began my daily Voice Expression practice. Before I knew how I would continue to use breath to heal and recover from trauma.

Fast-forward thirty years, and I find myself in a Transformational Breathwork session where we're breathing deeply and consistently. My body shakes, much like when I was in labor with my first child. My belly heaves with emotions. But I'm not alone. I have a practitioner and other loving people there with me. I'm able to release these deep emotions—through tears, wailing, vocal toning, and the breath itself.

After this release, I felt lighter. I could breathe much more easily and completely.

I realized that my voice work all these years has been a type of breathwork. I've been breathing and easing my past traumas. I've been healing my body with my own voice.

Let's Play!

Journal Play

Have you found power in your breath?

Write about any times when you've found your breath. Or lost your breath.

Do you notice how you breathe during the day? Is it shallow? Or do you breathe deeply?

When you do your Voice Expression practice, what do you notice about your breathing? Do you get short of breath? Or does it deepen?

Sound Play

Let's use this time to tune in to your breath. We've done other breath practices, but let's try something a little bit different.

Take a moment to notice how you're breathing. Try not to change anything. Without judging yourself, notice what's happening as you inhale. And as you exhale. What do you notice? What do you feel?

You can move into "box breathing," as we did earlier in this book. Inhale as you count slowly to four. Pause for four. Exhale for four. Pause for four. Repeat for four cycles. Then allow your breath to equalize, noticing your breathing again.

- Has it changed?
- Is it slower?
- More relaxed?

- Do you notice if your belly is expanding?
- Or is your chest expanding?
- Do you start with the belly and then the chest?

If you don't feel your belly expanding, lay your hands on your belly. Allow the weight of your hands and arms to support your sensations.

As you inhale, does your belly rise into your hands? This is easier to feel when lying on your back; perhaps you'd like to try that if you aren't already doing so.

Take some time to breathe into your belly and notice it lowering as you exhale. If you don't feel this, you can try lying on your belly to feel the expansion and compression of the belly with each breath.

Maybe you want to breathe in through your mouth and out through your mouth, relaxing on the exhale.

Then allow the breath to fill your belly and continue up into your chest, relaxing as you exhale.

Keep cycling your breath without any pauses.

Add a sound on the exhale. Maybe the heart chakra sound of "aw." Or, if you feel another sound wanting to come, allow that. Let it out as loudly as you desire, until you feel complete with the sound. Then return to your usual breathing cycle. Breathing in. Breathing out. Breathing in. Breathing out.

There may be more sounds that want to come. Allow them. And return to the breath again.

Continue for as much time as you'd like.

When you feel ready to come to completion, allow your breath to return to normal. Bring your awareness back to your fingers and toes. Open your eyes and stretch your body. Come back fully into your body and into your space.

Now share in your journal how you're feeling.

Playing in Business

When you're feeling stuck or frustrated in your business, you can do the above exercise for a short period. It may reignite you. Or calm you.

What are the areas in your business that have you stuck? Can you identify them?

Use the "7 Proven Steps" checklist (see Appendix C) to feel into those areas that feel stuck or frustrating.

What is it that you don't know?

If you knew how to do that, how would that help you move forward?

2. Shine Your Light

When a hand-analysis session showed that I was an "Artist in the Spotlight" and that my Natural Genius was Performing, my first thought was, *How could that be? I have stage fright!* Moments later, I felt a sense of shame around having attention on me as I perform.

However, as I spent time unpacking those aspects of myself, this idea that I'm meant to be in the spotlight and standing on stage made sense. I'd always wanted attention and wanted to perform. But when I got that attention, especially when I was on stage, I would freeze.

Now I understand that freezing is a response to fear. And as I look into the reaction, I see that my true reaction was "faint" (a slightly different response to fear—more on that later).

What was I afraid of? Growing up, I didn't feel safe to be seen or heard. As I learned more about the disease of alcoholism, I saw that this is a common experience of adult children of alcoholics. We learn it's not safe to speak about anything that goes on in the home. I learned it wasn't safe to speak up in my own home either.

So, could this genius of performing look different from standing on stage with the spotlight on me? Could it be how I show up in my life? I played with that a lot. And yes, it is very much about the energy of performing. It's about how I show up in the world. Do I show up in the light? Apparently, I do without even trying, as people have shared with me.

Isn't that what our Natural Genius feels like? According to Bill Lamond in his coaching program, Fulfillment-Based Thinking, "Natural Genius is when we're doing the thing that nobody taught us, that we've always known how to do, and when we do it, we feel fulfilled and on purpose." When I show up and feel myself shining, then I'm performing. My life is my stage. And the light of Source Energy is my spotlight.

What about you? Have you had trouble showing up fully in your life? Do you know your Natural Genius? What stops you from expressing that genius? Is it fear?

When I started telling people that my Natural Genius was performing, many of them encouraged me to audition for one of our local community plays. I was petrified, having been traumatized in high school by auditioning for a musical. But with the encouragement of knowing my Natural Genius and a bit of hand-holding from my friends, I showed up at an audition. Sometimes our fears aren't so big and important that having support can't help us overcome them.

I tried out for that play. I got a role. I learned so much about memorizing lines and getting into character and building a character's backstory. I met others who have done lots of acting, and I really soaked in the joy I felt being on stage and in the spotlight. I found myself feeling at home on stage. And backstage. I continued to audition for plays, and I got a role almost every time. I've also made lifelong friends in the process.

I faced that huge fear of auditioning and performing in a play. But my genius of performing goes beyond that. I'm called to be a speaker on stage. I'm no longer afraid of being on stage or in the spotlight. I'm getting clearer on the message I'm speaking about. And I feel closer and closer to having that vision come to life. In fact, I'm seeing glimpses of it as I speak and perform my form of sound healing in front of audiences more and more. It may not be the big stage or the full auditorium yet, but I know wholeheartedly that it is coming.

Are you ready to perform your life? You don't need to do it alone. I had friends walk with me into that audition. And now I have coaches and programs that support me on my journey forward. What support system do you have in place? If you don't have one, how could you bring in more support?

Let's Play!

Journal Play

In your journal, explore:

- What does it mean to "perform your life"?
- Where do you shine in your life?
- Where do you shy away?
- What part of your vision scares you?

Sound Play

Remember the solar plexus sound?

We've played with this sound before (in "I Feel Shushed" and "Do I Need to Know What Pitch I'm Singing?"). Yet here we are again because feeling empowered to perform your life takes feeling empowered within yourself. The solar plexus is where we express our true self fully.

The sound is "oh." The color is yellow (or gold).

Go to your safe space and play with the "oh" sound as you see yourself showing up fully in your life.

Can you feel your body opening as you make this sound?

Are your shoulders starting to relax?

Notice the sound of your "oh." Is it big and loud? Or quiet and small? No need to judge yourself for the sound your voice is making. Allow it.

As you repeat the "oh" sound, notice how it's shifting and soothing you.

Consider offering yourself to your fullest expression in this sound practice. And if you aren't doing a daily Voice Expression practice, I encourage you to consider doing it. It could be just one sound. This "oh" is a great one. Or two or three sounds. You could choose the ones that you need in that moment.

Or maybe consider taking five to ten minutes each day to make the sounds of all twelve chakras in my Voice Expression practice. See how you feel after a week of doing it daily. After two weeks. Can you test this out over twenty-one to thirty days? It takes time to create a new habit.

In order to fully express yourself and perform your life, your solar plexus chakra and the "oh" sound can support you.

No matter which daily practice you choose to do, you are doing it right for you. And that's all that matters.

Playing in Business

In my "7 Proven Steps" program, performing is what I call "shine." It aligns with the solar plexus chakra and the color yellow.

In business, we're called to shine in many ways:

- On camera – to teach, promote, and share on social media.
- On stage – to teach, promote, and connect with your ideal divine clients.
- In photos – to use in promotional materials.
- In writing – for emails, social media posts, books, and teaching materials.

We make offers for our services in many ways.

Spend a few moments using the sound "oh" to feel into how you feel about "going live" on camera, on stage, or in other ways.

What's coming up for you?

- Fears?
- Do you want to run away?
- Do you freeze?

- Do you want to hide?
- Do you want to fight against this concept?
- Do you feel confused? Is that stopping you?

Fears are often a sign that we're going in the right direction. However, it's not comfortable to face them. You may already know there's usually some discomfort involved in growing.

Use the sound of your voice to soothe these fears and to bring in your personal power. Trust that if you've been guided by something greater than yourself to do your healing work, you're fully supported in doing it. And remember that you don't have to do it alone. You're allowed to ask for help.

3. Shift Your Energy

Are you a healer?

I'd venture to say we're all healers in the sense that when we cut ourselves, our bodies can heal themselves. And, on an emotional level, I'm sure you've helped others by saying something when they were struggling. Has that happened to you?

When I began my healing journey with an energy healer, she helped me realize that I'm a healer. I was in my forties, and I'd never experienced this type of healing before. I didn't consider myself spiritual in any way, yet I felt like I was coming home to myself. I came to understand I've always been spiritual. I've always been a healer. I just didn't know it because I didn't have the context for the gifts I had.

Awakening my voice in those sessions showed me the gift that we all have in our voice—and that, ultimately, we're all healers.

I later became attuned as a Reiki Practitioner and eventually as a Reiki Master. I also developed my own sound healing modality called Sound Washing and then became a certified yoga teacher. The certifications seemed to confirm something that was in me even without those certificates. I felt called to get those certifications, but I know we can be healers even without them.

When I ask if you're a healer, you may have different feelings and thoughts around who is a healer and whether you are one. If you call yourself a healer or resonate with that term for yourself, then keep reading. If you don't necessarily feel like a healer but have some understanding of chakras (what you read in the first section is enough), read on.

This chapter is about energy—specifically, the seven major chakras, and how we can use our voice to shift the energy of a chakra. We've been working with these seven major chakras already, so feel free to explore this technique for yourself. And if you're interested in helping others with this, I can help you begin your journey as a healer or to take the next step in that direction. Reach out here: phoebe@phoebefazio.com.

As we use our voice to vibrate our chakras, we're tapping into each chakra and tuning in to the sensations of that energy center. Just by making the sound, we can shift and align the energy flow.

Let's Play!

Sound Play

Here are some other techniques I've played with and found to be quite powerful.

Let's say you're doing your daily practice of toning each chakra and you come across one that feels tight in your throat. It feels hard to make sound. Maybe the sound is gravelly or just very quiet. First things first, try not to make judgments, like deciding you're getting a cold or that there's some other reason why your voice is sounding/feeling that way.

After noticing this, you might use your voice to bring the energy of another chakra that *is* feeling good to support the one that's not. The heart chakra is often where I start, but any chakra will serve the purpose.

For example, let's say your throat chakra is tight. You could:

- Tune in and make the sound of the heart chakra ("aw") and then let the pitch rise up a bit to the level of the voice so that you're making the "aw" sound up where the throat chakra lives. You may want to do that sliding from heart to throat a few times. Take it easy, gently moving the heart energy up to the throat. Then, as you feel the throat filling with more energy flow, try the throat again with the "ay" sound. See if there's been a shift.
- You can also try bringing a higher chakra down. In some cases, it takes both. I love bringing the crown chakra down, for instance, as the divine energy is so soothing.
- Another way to use your voice to heal a chakra is to put the challenged chakra in the middle and tone through three chakras. In the case of the throat, start with the heart chakra ("aw") and then move to the throat ("ay") and up

to the brow ("eye"). Slide from low to high and then down from high to low, as if you were massaging through these three chakras.

As an energy healer, I do this on the body with my hands, or just above the body. If you're familiar with this technique, then you can do the same basic thing with your voice—moving the energy with the sounds of your own voice.

Always go back to the original challenged chakra to check and see if a change has happened.

Journal Play

Write about your experience with your sound play above.

- Which chakra did you find was out of balance?
- Which other chakras did you use to support this one?
- What did you notice?

Playing in Business

Whether or not you're a healer in business for yourself, working in another setting, or just healing yourself, healing a chakra can be useful.

In my business program, I guide healers through the different chakras for their business. When one of those areas is out of alignment or out of balance, we can use the techniques described above to play with the sound to bring it back into alignment.

When all parts of our business are flowing with ease, we're able to thrive. We feel that our work is sustainable—no overworking or under-earning.

You can use the "7 Proven Steps" checklist (Appendix C) to tune in to the seven parts of your business. Check in to see where you're doing well and where the challenges are for you. You can then use your voice to assist with balancing these parts of your business.

4. How You Can Add Your Voice to Your Healing Work

I'd been playing with sounds that came out of my mouth since I found my healing voice that I use in my Sound Washings. I decided to teach others how to use their voice in a toning class. During that class, some of the students asked if we could see what would happen if we combined the sounds with Reiki. So, after class one evening, a few students who were Reiki practitioners took turns lying on the table and receiving sounds and Reiki combined.

It was so powerful and gorgeous. Everyone had different experiences, and the sounds that came out were amazing.

The support of toning together as we did the Reiki was incredible. I didn't have the courage to trust in doing that for my own Reiki sessions before then. But after that experiment, I was able to do it. I tested it out on every Reiki client who came to me. And it became what I do.

Now my Reiki sessions always include Sound Washing. When I put my hands on my client, the sounds bubble up and out of my mouth. It's effortless. I could do it for hours without any strain. I feel like I don't even need to breathe. Even when I do distant sessions, the sounds come through and people report feeling the vibrations.

I believe that when I learned to open the channel for Universal Love and Light, as in Reiki, I also opened the sacred sound channel/current. I asked for support from light beings, so I've received amazing beings who voice through me. Sometimes these light beings even come together.

One day I was doing a mini session in a fire-relief situation after our town had lost so much from a harsh wildfire. In that session, I was playing a bowl and making my sounds over a man. At the end of the session, he opened his eyes and said he was surprised to see only me. He thought there was an entire choir of angels and other light beings making those sounds. I believe there were. They were coming through my voice. I too am in awe of what comes through my voice.

These experiences—along with sharing online, over the phone, via Zoom, and on videos—gave me more courage to use my voice for healing. One of my mentors asked me why I wasn't toning in front of our local Center for Spiritual Living. So I offered to do just that. They were offering a two-minute meditation, and once a month I would do a Sound Washing during those two minutes. I set the intention for the length of time, and it was always the exact right length and message that people needed to hear.

The courage came not just from the experiences of using my voice in Reiki sessions and having a mentor to encourage me, but also with daily Voice Expression practice, which strengthened me in such a gentle way. I found myself more grounded, more connected to the Divine, and more balanced and aligned in my own energy system.

Somehow, while making these sounds that seemed so strange to me, I was healing myself.

Let's Play!

Journal Play

As you've been going through this book, have you considered adding your voice to your healing work? Do you already use your voice in your form of healing? How do you use it?

If you've wanted to add your voice to your healing work, are you willing to give it a try?

If you've already tried adding your voice to your healing work, what happened? What did you notice? What did your clients notice? Will you do it some more?

As usual, I suggest you share in your journal or with your accountability partner. Allow them to be a support for you as you are for them.

Sound Play

When I begin a Reiki and Sound Washing session, I usually start with a spoken affirmative prayer with my hands on my client's shoulders as I stand behind them (while they're lying on the table). Then I move my hands to gently cup their eyes. That's usually when the sounds begin.

I begin with a gentle hum and notice what my mouth does. In the beginning of testing this out, the "uh" sound came first. I could feel myself grounding as I made that sound of the root chakra.

I stayed with that sound for as long as it felt right. Sometimes I moved my hands, and the sound stayed the same. Other times, the sound changed before I moved. I tried to let myself feel and follow the flow of the energy and the sensations in my throat as the sounds flowed.

If you don't have a person to try this out with, you can try it with a pet. Or go outside in nature. Put your hands on a tree. Try the "uh" sound to start and see what comes. Or pick up a rock and do the same type of thing.

You might even sit on the grass and put your hands flat on the earth and make the sound that connects us to the earth: "uhhhhh."

Once you feel grounded, you can move to a new sound as it occurs to you. You don't have to go in order of the chakras, but you can. If you're working with a person, you could make the sounds of their chakras as you place your hands on each one. But I invite you to stay open and willing for the sounds to come in different ways.

Consider allowing sounds that you've never made before to come out through your voice. Stay grounded and relaxed in the process. You could try recording yourself so you can hear it afterward. You may surprise yourself.

Allow silence as well. This process isn't about inundating anyone with lots of sounds. It's about being sensitive and offering the healing vibrations of your voice to support the person, animal, or item.

It's all an experiment. You can't hurt anyone unless you scream in their ear or do something harsh like that. If you're grounded and tuned in, you'll provide just the right healing sounds that combine with your healing modality.

After your session, allow your client time to integrate the sounds and healing. When they're ready, ask if they can share some of what they experienced. And you can share what you felt to support them further. I find that what I notice and what my clients notice tend to connect when we talk afterward.

Playing in Business

We addressed the root chakra in the first section as we found our safe places to make sounds with our voices—and then when we added consonants to the vowel sounds of the chakras and the Voice Expression practice.

Now let's come back to that chakra—to the "uh" sound, the color red, and the sense of safety and security.

As you consider adding sound to your healing work, and as you tune in to your platform for your business, spend some time sitting with the sound of your voice. Allow the "uh" sound to come. Nice and easy. Low and slow.

Perhaps add in some consonants. Play with the sensations of consonants with the "uh": buh, buh, buh… duh, duh, duh… tuh, tuh, tuh… kuh, kuh, kuh… muh, muh, muh. Close your eyes and let your mouth move.

As you make these sounds, tune in to your work in this world.

Tune in to where you're standing strong.

Tune in to where your potential clients find you.

Acknowledge all that you've already done in your business with respect to your platform—where you're standing.

And ask for the Divine white light from above to come in to illuminate your root chakra and to guide you to your next step for your business. What's your next step to be more secure with where you're showing up?

Notice what comes up for you when you're grounded and this unconditional love and support of the Divine is guiding you. You can't do this wrong, and whatever comes has value. Accept it and go from there.

- What do you feel?
- Do you feel empowered?
- Do you feel fear?
- Do you want to distract yourself?
- Do you feel anger and frustration?

Whatever you feel, write about it. Or talk about it or express it the way that calls to you.

5. Allow Your Voice to Help Others

Have you ever considered that other people could be comforted by your voice? Has anyone ever told you that the sound of your voice is soothing? Did you know that your voice could be healing to others?

I never thought my voice was soothing to anyone. As a child, I didn't think my voice mattered. In choirs, I felt like just one of the crowd, not essential. As a teacher, I learned how to have an authoritative voice. I had that modeled for me in my family and all through school.

When I found my new voice, many people told me I'd help others with it. At first, I was curious about what that meant and how that would look. Now I find it reassuring when people comment on how calming and soothing my voice is, and I find ways to use it for healing.

The obvious ways my voice is healing are in my Reiki/Sound Washing healing sessions where I use my voice intuitively as one of my many sound healing instruments. I also perform Sound Washings with specific healing intentions.

The not-so-obvious ways are when I'm talking with someone on the phone. Maybe it's because I'm relaxed and know how to use my voice in a relaxed manner that causes people to feel that sense of calm. On a microphone, I'm relaxed and enjoy hearing the quality of my own voice. And others comment that my voice sounds meditative. I can lead trainings and coaching calls that help people easily learn the challenging technologies and systems involved in growing their healing business. This is helpful to them, as many of my clients are nervous about such things.

I've come to understand that when we heal our voice, it has the potential to heal others. We can't force that to happen. I imagine that many people don't realize they can change the quality of their voice to become healing for others.

Have you ever wanted your voice to be soothing? Did you know you could do some simple techniques to heal your own voice so that it can soothe others?

I wonder if we think it's more about *what* we say that matters. Is it really the words we say? Or is it *how* we say the words? Is it the sound and quality of our voice that's soothing and healing?

Let's Play!

Journal Play

The Voice Expression practice I've shared with you is much more than healing your own voice (although it is that). It's also a vehicle for balancing your energy and aligning yourself with the Divine and your divine gifts. And it's useful in many other ways that only you will experience when you test it out.

I invite you to explore:

- How can you heal your voice?
- What's helped so far?
- What have you avoided trying?
- What does it mean to heal your own voice?
- What needs healing?
- Do you want to help others with your voice?
- What would that feel like?
- In what ways do you see this working in your life?

Sound Play

To help you determine whether your voice is already healing for others or there's more for you to explore, let's play with a few sounds.

We've played with the throat chakra sound "ay." Let's return there.

Take a few gentle breaths and allow the sound of your throat chakra to float out. Feel into what your throat has to say to you. Feel the sensations. Notice the quality of the sound without any judgment. Just noticing it.

Then let's also play with the solar plexus sound of "oh." As before, tune in to the sensations and the quality of the sounds.

Now let's call on the Divine and make the sound of the crown chakra, "ee," again, tuning in to the sensations.

Follow your intuition for any other sounds that wish to be played through your voice. Trust where you're guided.

Maybe you feel guided to move through all the chakras in order, from root to crown or maybe from crown to root. Or perhaps you're called to use the twelve chakras—all of them or just specific ones.

As you play with the sounds, see what's being shown to you.

What are you hearing, seeing, or feeling about your voice and how it helps others?

What are you feeling about whether or not you want to use your voice to help others?

How might that look? Using these sounds for others? Recording guided meditations? Singing? Speaking?

Playing in Business

When we're looking at using our voice to help others, how does that apply to our business as a healer?

In my "7 Proven Steps," the heart chakra is the place where we're of service. And our voice is used to share with others and to provide the actual service.

Let's play with the sounds of the heart chakra and high heart chakra (the upper chest between heart and throat chakras): "aw" and "ah." Call on the colors of green and turquoise.

Tune in to how you're of service.

- In what ways do you use your voice in your service work?
- Talking with clients?
- Toning with clients?
- Speaking prayers or affirmations?

- Guided meditations?
- Videos?

Now play with the sound of your throat chakra ("ay") and see what wants to be expressed about how your voice is healing for others.

You can also tap into more of the twelve chakras, such as your soul star ("ih"), the earth star ("mm-vv-zz"), and the cranial ("ng").

With each of these sounds, ask the same questions about how your voice is healing for others. Note the answers in your journal.

6. Discover the Healing Power of Your Voice

Have you ever imagined using your own voice to heal your voice? What about using your voice to heal your body? I didn't know this was possible until it started happening to me.

Don Campbell's audiobook *Healing Yourself with Your Own Voice* inspired me to use my voice to heal myself. From there, I was guided to start my journey with a practice that would align my chakras.

I did a bit of research into different ways to align the chakras and was guided to use my voice to do that. I came across a few different systems. One used vowels and the other used seed mantras, called "bija mantras." I love them both and chose to use the vowels (which you can learn about in Jonathan Goldman's *Vocal Toning the Chakras*).

Within the vowel system of toning the chakras, there were different systems as well. I chose the one that aligned with my own energy system—in other words, the one that felt best when I did it. And then I ended up switching the order of a couple of the sounds (again, after tuning in to my body and feeling what was best for me).

This practice of toning the seven chakras was my introduction to healing my own body with my voice. And you can use it as well, if it feels good to you.

Over time, I noticed how good I felt after doing that practice each day. I could feel my energy aligning. I could feel my body gaining strength, my mind calming, and my emotions coming into a balanced state of calm. I also noticed that I wasn't getting sick as often, I slept better, I ate better without trying, and I was able to hear and follow guidance with ease. Basically, I got out of my own way.

After years of doing this daily Voice Expression practice, I received guidance to tune in to the twelve-chakra system—the basis for my current Voice Expression practice. I've been doing this one for the past few years, and it's really upleveled my practice and my life.

Are you working with the twelve-chakra system? I was guided to tune in during the 12/12 portal between December 12 and December 21. The synchronicity of those numbers/dates made this guidance even more powerful. The sounds that came through and the new chakras I discovered were all so supportive for me.

At that time, I was living with my aging mother, who I took care of until her passing. I was also growing my business and supporting my youngest adult child as they were suicidal and needed to come home for help. I faced many other difficulties during this time, but this toning of the twelve chakras carried me through with strength and grace.

I found that after doing this twelve-chakra toning, I'd often play with more sounds, which I later came to understand is my own unique form of sound healing called Sound Washing.

Let's Play!

Journal Play

I invite you to reflect on these questions and write your answers (or related thoughts) in your journal.

- What do you want to heal in your body, mind, emotions, or spirit?
- What's shifting over time as you use your voice for healing?
- Have you been using the Voice Expression practice?
- Did you try the seven chakras? What about the twelve chakras?
- If you've tried both, is one feeling better for you?
- Are you feeling guidance to make other sounds?
- Have you been practicing daily?
- How do you feel as a result?
- What questions are coming up for you?

Sound Play

Let's play with sounds that will support you.

I recommend beginning with one of the Voice Expression practices we've already discussed. If you've been doing it, then let's do this next exercise after you've done your daily practice.

After your own Voice Expression practice, choose a chakra to focus on here. Or you can choose anything you'd like to heal in yourself. Do you have any physical pain? Emotional upset? Anything in your life that you'd like to elevate?

If your life is already wonderful and you aren't able to identify anything you'd like to improve for yourself, I invite you to play with the Galactic Gateway chakra, using the sound "rr" and opening to your highest expression, perhaps while tuning in to your vision. What do you need in order to live that vision? You can go further into the vision using any practices in this book (or elsewhere).

As you explored your chakras, did you notice one that felt weaker? Is there a chakra that didn't sound as clear, strong, and easy as the others? This can guide you toward what you wish to choose for this practice.

Once you've selected one chakra (or another focus), tune in to that area and make the sound for that chakra. (If it's not a chakra, ask your voice what sound would be appropriate for this condition.) Gently, and without judgment, notice the feeling before you make the sound. It may help to write this down so you can compare at the end.

As you make the sound, repeating it and breathing fully in between, feel into the deeper meaning of that chakra. Get curious.

- What comes up for you?
- Are there emotions? Physical sensations?
- What's underneath that?
- Is it a memory? Fear?

As you identify a bit more of what's going on, allow the sound to soothe you.

Keep making the sound if you can, even if tears are coming.

Keep making gentle sound, even if it doesn't sound "good."

Keep making the sound.

Keep breathing.

Play with a different pitch: higher, lower.

Play with the volume: louder, quieter.

Stay with the sound until you feel a shift.

After the shift, bring your sound practice to a close.

Spend some time in the silence, then feel what's different. What's changed within you?

Remember what you felt before starting?

The power of your voice for your own healing is limitless.

I encourage you to repeat this practice anytime you'd like to improve or elevate something in your life.

I also encourage you to share about what you're experiencing, whether it's healing results, frustrations, hesitations, or anything else. If this was your first time doing the Voice Expression practice, please share about that. Or, if you've been doing the Voice Expression practice regularly, mention that before you share how you were able to shift something in your life. Write in your journal or talk with your accountability partner about what you shifted.

Playing in Business

Just as you did for your own body or personal life, you can scan through your business chakras to see where you'd like to focus the healing power of your own voice.

You can find the checklist of the "7 Proven Steps" in Appendix C. See the link there to download the colorful checklist (and print it if you'd like) and use it to scan the different parts of your business. Then do your Voice Expression practice for your business.

Tune in to each aspect of your business, as you can see on the checklist. Feel, listen, and get curious about what areas are needing a bit of attention.

- What have you been avoiding?
- What do you need more information about?
- What's holding you back?

Write this down.

Then make the sound for the related chakra.

Stay with that sound. Feel the emotions, the physical sensations, the thoughts, the memories, and all related experiences. Continue to stay with it as you keep breathing deeply on your inhale and making the sound on the exhale.

Continue until you feel a clear shift or you feel complete.

- What was the shift?
- How do you feel now?
- What's different from what you wrote at the beginning?
- Do you feel able to ask for the help you need? Or get moving on a task you have felt stuck on?

7. Open Yourself to More Sounds After the Chakras

Have you been playing with the Voice Expression practice? What have you been noticing? Does it feel easier as you do it more? Are you noticing a difference in your ability to speak? Or sing? Or express yourself in other ways?

Are you ready to play a little more?

If you've been making the sounds of each of the twelve chakras, you may be curious about what you could do with these sounds.

After I discovered the extra five chakras that make up the twelve-chakra system, I found myself playing with these newer sounds quite often. Sometimes I'd make a chakra sound and then move it from the original chakra to another, changing the pitch, just to see what that felt like.

Other times, I'd play with the vowels and see what it would be like to sound out certain words. Where would the sounds of a certain word fall in terms of the chakras?

And other times, I'd find that my mouth wanted to make new sounds.

Let's Play!

Sound Play

Here's a fun technique I've enjoyed that helped me become increasingly open to making more sounds with my voice. I call it "Word Play."

When I played with words and the chakra sounds, I was taken in a new direction. The thing about words is that there are so many hidden sounds in them. Let's take the word *awake*, for example. The sounds of this word could be broken down into these sounds: "uh-oo-ay-ee-k." Even though there are few vowels in the written word, when we speak it and slow down our speech, we discover even more sounds. The *w* sound is made up of "oo," and the following *a* is made up of "ay" and "ee."

Now let's look at where those sounds lie in the twelve-chakra system: "uh" (root), "oo" (sacral), "ay" (throat), "ee" (crown). So we could move from root, up to sacral, then to the throat, and followed by the crown. As we repeat this pattern, check in with how the sounds change and if you feel a change in your physical body, emotions, or thoughts.

What word comes to you to try? Break down every single vowel sound as much as you can. Write down the sounds and find the chakras that go with them.

When we play like this, we keep our mind open to receiving, curious about what we might experience. Enjoy playing and wondering what comes of it.

I enjoy playing with affirmations this way. One that I've had a lot of fun with is *I am* ("ah-ee-ah-mm"): high heart-crown-heart-Earth Star. Try it for yourself.

Om is also full of more sounds than I ever imagined. In fact, I found all twelve of the sounds inside the *Om* sound. Try it for yourself. Can you find all twelve? Now I understand what people mean when they say that *Om* is the sound of all sounds of the universe inside the one sound.

Playing in Business

You can use this process in your business as well.

Are there words, phrases, or affirmations you use with your clients? Play with those.

What about having a fun time playing with the chakra sounds of your business?

Use the "7 Proven Steps" checklist again (Appendix C) to identify the parts of your business and how they align with the chakras.

Make the sound for the stronger parts of your business, then move that into the other areas to strengthen those aspects of your business.

You can play with this concept of using your voice to play with the sounds that will empower you and your business so that you can help more people with your healing gifts and your voice.

And remember to keep playing and having fun. You didn't start this business to have another "job," did you? (Sometimes we forget that.)

8. Protect Your Voice

Have you ever had laryngitis? Lost your voice? Had trouble speaking or singing due to physical constraints in your throat?

I'm not a doctor and cannot diagnose or treat any medical conditions, so if you have any issues with your throat, please consult your doctor. However, I can say that when you're doing any vocal practice, it's important to approach it with loving kindness. Be gentle with how you use your voice. What is gentle? Only you will know this. Making quiet sounds can sometimes be harder on the voice than louder ones, but making louder sounds can be harsh as well.

If you approach the practice in a relaxed manner, you'll most likely get the best results. Good, deep breathing. Relaxed shoulders, facial muscles, jaw, and neck. Notice the way your body feels while you're making the sounds with your voice. Remind yourself to go easy.

When I feel more like I'm playing, I notice new abilities in my voice. For example, I can hold a tone longer by not trying.

My most profound lesson in the value of relaxing, playing, and not forcing sounds came from my experiences with overtones. You can read my story about how I learned about these fascinating sounds in the chapter "Overtone Chanting and Even Higher Realms" (in the next section), but for now, understand that overtones are created when one person vocalizes a tone and, through special techniques, the sound is divided, creating more than one pitch. It might seem impossible that one person could create two different pitches simultaneously through their single voice, but it's true.

I was intrigued by hearing other people making these overtones, but imagine my surprise when I heard them coming from my own voice!

I started to notice that I was making overtone sounds when I was in group settings and also when working with private clients on the table. But when I tried to replicate these sounds during my voice practice, it was a struggle. Despite my efforts, I couldn't force it to happen.

I wondered how I could make the overtones whenever I wanted to and have them dance around me, as I'd experienced before from others. So I studied, learned, practiced, and played with many techniques until I could do it on command. It took a lot of practice and patience and letting go of the effort. (I'll share with you the exact steps so you can learn how to do it too.) Now I find that it comes most naturally when it feels easy and fun.

If you're trying to make something happen, I invite you to let it go. Let go of the expectations. Let go of how or when it will happen. Open yourself to the possibility that you'll be guided to the techniques and that, through play and fun, it will come to you.

Please care for your voice. It's precious. And when you feel discomfort, stop, rest, drink some water, and come back to it another time. Maybe another day. Never push through. It's not worth the risk. Healing from vocal conditions takes a long time and lots of vocal rest (no talking, singing, or toning), so it's best to avoid causing any strain.

The practices I share in this book are meant to be enjoyable and enlightening. Allow them to happen freely. And please take good care of yourself as you learn more about yourself in the process.

It is with love that I encourage you to play with sound with your voice. If it feels like a struggle, maybe you could use a guide to ease your way with this.

Have you noticed the titles I use?

- Let's Play
- Journal Play
- Sound Play
- Playing in Business

This is why I decided to title these sections in this way—to keep it light and welcoming.

As I've shared earlier, our throat is such a tender part of our body. Even coughing can cause it some harm. So stay hydrated. If you do cough before making sound, please swallow a few times to soothe that harsh strain on your vocal cords.

Check in with your experiences during your voice practice:

- Have you felt any strain in the practices?

- Have you noticed it getting easier over time to make sound with your voice?
- Is your voice changing as you do these practices?
- Do you feel your confidence improving around using your voice?
- How about the other ways you express yourself? Any changes there?

If you'd like to share about anything you've experienced on your journey of making sound with your voice throughout this book, please do share—with your accountability partner, with me, or with anyone else you feel drawn to share with.

9. Joining Voices in Community

Have you been wondering about making some of these sounds in community? Do you have a community of people who might be interested? Have you ever toned together with others? Have you sung in groups before? Choirs? Church? Singing groups?

When I first discovered my new voice, I wanted to share it. I didn't really know how to, but after reading the book *Toning* by Laurel Elizabeth Keyes, I found the courage to invite people to my house for a toning circle. Anyone can do that.

People came. And it was so much fun. Everyone got something from it. And I loved hosting and leading these circles. I still enjoy them.

As I did my daily Voice Expression practice, I started to share about it. And the best way for me to share it was to invite others to do it with me. So I shared at church, Tai Chi classes, meditation circles, yoga classes, and other places where I felt that people would be open and willing to try this type of voice practice.

In some of those groups, I began to share my Sound Washing too. That's a different story, but it took the same kind of courage to offer myself in that way.

I understand that not everyone wants to host their own circles. Maybe there's a place near you that's doing something similar where you can join them or share some of what you're learning in this book.

There's something very special that happens when we make these sounds with others. I find a freedom that I don't always feel when I'm alone. When I tone with others, I find new sounds as our voices join together. And the spiritual connections are deeper than when I'm just methodically going through each chakra tone with my own voice. It also sometimes leads to adventures with sound as we wander off the beaten path.

As we vibrate our voices together, we can feel the harmonies and the dissonances. The dissonance is often very cleansing and makes way for beautiful frequencies as a result of the release. I find it easier to embrace those dissonances with joy and delight when we're all playing together.

Have you wanted to make sounds with others? Have you tried it? Are you interested in starting your own circle?

You can use this book as a guide for ways you could lead one—or share the leadership role with others in creating a circle of like-minded people who'd like to play with the sounds of their voices.

VI. Advanced Voice Practices

1. Exploring the Upper Realms

Are you ready to play with sounds that can transport you upward? Have you ever played with angelic sounds with your voice? Have you ever wondered about overtone chanting?

After I'd been doing the Voice Expression practice with the seven major chakras for a while, for myself and teaching it to others, I realized how easily we could travel upward.

It's simple and yet so playful. When I got to the crown chakra ("ee"), I allowed my voice to explore higher pitches by floating up and down wherever my voice wanted to go. As I did that, I noticed that sometimes it felt like I was singing with the angels.

When I invited others to do this as well, we all had our own experience with playing with these upper vibrations, and together it felt like we were contacting the upper realms.

With the twelve chakras, you can also do this with the Soul Star chakra. Its sound, "ih," can help us access higher pitches with more ease. I encourage you to test it out and see where it takes you.

Let's Play!

Journal Play

Explore in your journal how it would feel to sing with the angels.

- What does it mean to you to access upper realms?
- Have you already found yourself accessing higher states of consciousness? With this voice and visioning work? Or some other ways?
- Is this something you're interested in experiencing more?

Sound Play

I recommend that you begin by doing your version of the Voice Expression practice (either seven or twelve chakras). Then, as you come to the crown (in either system), take a little more time and allow your voice to float up in pitch. It can float up and down a little bit at a time. Don't rush this. The magic is in the slow, subtle changes. (For a demonstration, please visit phoebefazio.com/book-extras.)

Then, if you'd like to try some more, move up to the Soul Star chakra above your head. Using the "ih" sound, allow your voice to do the same type of thing—floating up and down slowly.

I find that the "ih" sound and the energy of the Soul Star work together to bring me into a higher state. And as I continue, the sounds begin to lighten and feel more like angel sounds.

Remember to stay relaxed in your throat and neck. Breathe and move slowly. Allow the sounds to move up into your head rather than down to your chest. The more they're in your head, the lighter they'll become.

Tune in to the sensations. Keep breathing. You may find that you can continue your tones longer if you're truly accessing the lighter, higher vibrations.

Have fun playing here as long as you'd like. And be conscious of any discomfort or dryness in your throat. Don't push yourself. You can always come back for more later. Start with short sessions and expand gently as it becomes easier for you.

Playing in Business

Accessing these upper realms can assist you with your business.

Is accessing higher consciousness already part of your healing work? If so, then this will be fun for you.

You can use these angel sounds to guide you in making decisions in your business. You can ask for support from your angels and guides in this way.

Start with a question you have for your business (such as *Who is my divine ideal client?*), then do your Voice Expression practice and end it with this angelic sound practice. See what comes to you.

The answer may surprise you. Or it may be something you knew but didn't have the confidence to move forward with.

I often doubt my own intuition, but when I get confirmation, I feel confident enough to move forward. I know I can trust my guidance. And I feel safer moving forward knowing that it's for my highest expression and a way for me to help more people.

Did you get some answers? Clear guidance?

Where will you share the answers to these questions?

2. Overtone Chanting and Even Higher Realms

Have you heard of "overtone chanting"? Have you ever wondered how people do that? Have you tried to do it but found it impossible?

I experienced overtone chanting before I knew what it was. It started one day as I stood at the back of a dark auditorium watching a professional musician play his tambourine alone on stage. In addition to the tambourine, I was hearing high-pitched, beautiful, angelic, whisper singing that seemed to be coming from other places in the room, although there was no one else performing. It sounded like whistling, but I didn't know what it was. I looked back at the performer and tried to determine if he was making those beautiful, etheric sounds that danced around the room. How could he be? He looked like he was in a trance, and his mouth wasn't even moving.

It wasn't until years later when I heard those sounds again—this time from a musician at my spiritual center. After the service, I was able to ask him what that sound was. He called it overtone chanting. He didn't tell me how he did it, but at least I knew its name.

I later learned that this practice is also sometimes called overtoning, overtone singing, or Tuvan throat singing, but regardless of the name, it's based on the same thing: singing more than one tone at the same time.

As I was working with my Voice Expression practice and playing with what would later be called Sound Washing—on my own and in my healing sessions—I noticed that I was making those overtone sounds without even trying. I didn't know how it was happening, and I couldn't make it happen on purpose, but I was certainly interested.

So I went on a quest to discover what exactly this was and how to do it. I was led to books, videos, and live workshops about it. I finally found one technique that, after a lot of practice, enabled me to consistently create the overtones. Now I'd love to share that process with you.

Let's Play!

What Is Overtone Chanting?

Overtone chanting is when we're making and sustaining a tone with our voice and we're able to manipulate our tongue and mouth in a way that splits the sound. Splitting the sound is similar to playing harmonics on a guitar or blowing across the hole of a transverse flute (or the top of an open bottle); there are tones created in addition to the main tone we're starting with.

How Can I Learn to Do It?

As I mentioned, it took a long time and a lot of practice before I could consistently overtone at will. So, if you're new to this, please take your time, give yourself grace to not get it immediately, and keep trying. That's part of the process.

As we begin, it's important to be relaxed and to move slowly. Very slowly—even slower than you think—and then slower than that. At first, our mind wants to work hard at understanding, and our tongue wants to move quickly. But the slower and gentler you can be, the better it will go.

Here Are the Steps That Helped Me:

1. Find a tone you can sustain easily for a long time. If you aren't able to sustain one tone for a long time, then that's what you want to be working on before attempting anything else. (If you try it without being able to sustain a tone for a nice long time, you'll discover why I say this.)
2. To be able to hold a tone for longer, I suggest doing the Voice Expression practice daily, focusing on sustaining each tone. Notice how some are easier to sustain than others. Especially focus on sustaining on the "mm," "ng," and "rr" sounds.
3. Once you're able to sustain one tone using the above sounds with ease, you can start to play with very slow, subtle mouth movements. Starting with the "mm" move very slowly to the "oh" sound. Practice moving slowly

(very, very slowly) back and forth between the "mm" and the "oh." Pay attention to the sounds between the sounds. This could take a lot of practice. It might be days or weeks or months. Don't be in a rush.

4. Now we'll add another sound to the "mm" and the "oh." Again, moving as slowly as possible, add the "rr" sound. You may start to feel something at this point, but don't worry if you don't. Go as slowly as you possibly can. You'll feel like you're singing the word *more* in slow motion. Stay on the "rr" as you complete the sounds. Take note of where your tongue is when you're toning on the "rr." Can you feel that it's spread out? Can you feel the sides of your tongue touching your teeth? Also notice the corners of your mouth. Are they smiling? Can you create a tiny space in the center of your lips by pressing the outer corners together (as if you were drinking a thick milkshake through a straw)? Spend as much time as you'd like with this step. It takes time to develop these muscles and the awareness of your tongue and lips. Most of us don't spend much time contemplating these parts of our bodies.
5. Everything we've done so far can take time before you're ready for this next step. Again, no need to rush this. (And even if you do rush, that won't make it happen any sooner.)

6. Once you've developed the ability to sustain your tone through all the above steps and you still have the capacity to sustain the tone longer, you're ready to play with very slow movement of the tongue. To prepare, do some toning on "ee" and "oo" and notice the shape of your tongue. Can you sustain the "ee" sound and only change your lips to create the "oo"? If so, you may be feeling and hearing some of the overtone sensations. If not, this is where you want to play for a while. Again, it takes time to develop the sensations of the tongue and lips. Tune in. Take your time. If you aren't relaxed, give it a rest for now. Try again another time.
7. Now we're going to put it all together. Begin with the "more" sound in slow motion, and add the "ee-oo-ee-oo-ee-oo" for as long as you can sustain your tone. Draw in the corners of the lips toward each other (not toward the center). Create that small opening in the center of your lips with the outer corners drawn into a smile (not pursing your lips as in "oo"). Maintain that tension as you slowly change from the "ee" to the "oo" and back and forth with only your tongue moving inside your mouth. SLOWLY. VERY. VERY. SLOWLY.
8. Rest. Relax. Let it go. Stop trying so hard. It will come together when you're least expecting it. Let it be fun and playful.

9. When you're able to make these overtones, you may not even recognize it at first. It will feel different. You may feel new vibrations. You may feel a shift. You may hear something around you that isn't there when you stop. I didn't know I was doing it for sure until others told me they could hear it.
10. As you come into this sensation, allow yourself to feel the opening of the Galactic Gateway chakra. Open to the infinite number of chakras, higher dimensions, new realms. You may have reached them in other ways in the past, but this gives it a new dimension when you're vibrating your voice, your body, and your soul, feeling yourself elevated into these higher states.
11. Welcome to a new world.

Journal Play

Use your journal to express what happens as you try these techniques.

- What goes through your mind? What thoughts? What sensations?
- Are you feeling frustration? Tension?
- Have you tried going even slower?
- Have you started to feel a shift?
- Did you hear/feel the new sounds?
- Did you experience new dimensions? Are you getting glimpses?

- Have you felt elevated like this in the past? If so, when did you feel that before? What brought you there?

Share some of this in your journal or with your accountability partner or others.

Playing in Business

Can overtone chanting help us with our business?

The act of attempting this type of sound with your own voice is a lot like developing the entrepreneurial skills and mindset it takes to grow a healing business.

We're constantly reminded to come back to our own healing for ourselves and to remember why we're doing this in the first place.

Whether or not you can make these sounds, you're activating a part of you that wants to learn a new skill. And in the process, you're learning how to be in the beginner's mindset.

You can call on the Galactic Gateway with the sound of "rr." Imagine opening the gate a full arm's distance above your head. Allow the white, effervescent light to beam down through your crown, into your body, aligning and illuminating each of the chakras. Allow it to activate and align your entire being.

Then allow those vibrations to radiate out as you in your business.

Are you fully aligned?

Notice what you see, hear, and feel.

Are there areas that seem less illuminated? Can you bring more light to those darker, heavier areas?

When you complete this meditation in sound, go to your journal and write about the parts of your business associated with those chakras.

Which areas of your business need more attention? What stops you from expanding into those areas? What would it take to move forward with those areas?

Do you need more information? Do you need someone to talk to about it? Do you need guidance?

What have you realized about your healing work in the world through this process? Reach out for support from your accountability partner or maybe your toning circle.

VII. Deeper into Visioning

1. Notice It

"If your dream doesn't scare you, you don't have a dream, you have a plan."
– Rev. Deborah L. Johnson

Have you ever discovered that something in your life is exactly what you dreamed of? And then did you laugh when you realized that?

I noticed that in my life just recently.

Recently, I moved in with my boyfriend, now husband. The home where we live is in a small town about thirty miles away from where I'd been living for over twenty-five years. We have a beautiful, quiet, country life with tall evergreen trees (mostly pine, cedar, and fir) and wildlife that comes up to the house (deer, rabbits, squirrels, birds). I walk our private half-mile dirt road each morning and breathe in the fresh oxygen the trees provide and marvel at the tiny flowers that appear in spring after having just enough snow during the winter to enjoy without the hassle. We enjoy warm summers that aren't too hot and autumns that bring beautiful colored leaves.

I'd been enjoying this new life in the woods with my new husband for almost six months before it dawned on me that I'd imagined this life. When I moved to this area with my previous husband, this is the image I had. But the town where we were living was in a desert valley with high heat and no woods around us. It was a good life, but it wasn't what I was craving. That was thirty years ago, and now I'm living where I'd imagined—I'm living my vision!

What's your vision? If it's big enough, it may take a while. And it may scare you, especially if you knew it would take thirty years to come true. But don't give up on it.

Whatever your vision is, it's your highest vision if it has some of these elements:

- It's scaring you a bit.
- You're wondering how in the world you're going to make that your reality.
- You're willing to take as long as it takes to get there.

Now let's take steps toward living your vision. And remember, it can be fun!

Let's Play!

Journal Play

Consider the dreams you've attracted into your reality already. Celebrate those accomplishments. Write about them in your journal.

Here are some more steps you can take to help you keep noticing your vision and moving forward:

- Gather your support system around you. Make a list of people you can turn to. List them in your journal, your phone, an email list, a messenger group or Facebook group, or any other place where you'll see them.
- Do your daily self-care practices.
- Practice deep listening.
- Do your Voice Expression practice consistently.
- Tune in to your vision daily and feel how it feels to be in it fully.
- Take action toward your vision every day.

When you start to doubt yourself (and we all doubt ourselves at some point), have your support system remind you and hold you and keep you on your path.

Being in community with others who are living their vision or moving toward it is very powerful and supportive.

You don't have to do the scary stuff alone.

2. Merging Vision with Now

Have you ever noticed how time can collapse? Have you felt the fact that time is a construct?

We can do more when we trust in infinite time. I call on "angel time" a lot. When I'm late getting somewhere, I'll ask for angel time to help me. It works. Sometimes I get there in an amount of time that seems impossible. Other times the event doesn't start on time or the person I was meeting needed more time. And sometimes it turns out no one even noticed that I was late.

Another thing to consider is the manifesting technique of acting as if you have it now. Acting "as if" gives us the felt sense in our bodies that our vision is already happening right here, right now. It really works in bringing our dreams into reality!

I encourage you to look at your vision and notice what parts of it are already in your life in some way. They may not look exactly the way they did in your vision, but pay attention to them. Is there something that could shift in order for you to feel more like the way you do in your vision?

For example, my vision of standing on stage in front of a full auditorium is already happening in my life. I give live talks in person and online. As I share my story and teach about the power of voice in growing a healing business, I point out that I AM living my vision of standing on stage and speaking.

Remember that part of my story where I didn't know what I was doing on stage? As I do more and more speaking and acting "as if," it's become clear that I'm speaking about the voice. And YOU are my audience.

When I asked my future self, her wisdom showed me that I was writing books. So I'm taking action in that way as well, right here, right now. And writing this book helped me clarify my message in my speaking.

And you can do that too.

Let's Play!

Journal Play

Share in your journal and with your accountability partner about your experience of bringing aspects of your vision into this very moment.

- What are you already doing?
- What do you see in your life now that's like your vision?
- What are you bringing into your experience now that moves you closer to your vision?

Sound Play

Use your Voice Expression practice to help you see what's already here.

As you make each sound, feel the sensations of your vision.

Feel each chakra.

Feel each part of your physical being. Which sensations that you feel in your present moment are also in your vision?

What are those sensations? Excitement? Joy? Fulfillment?

Describe them in your journal after your practice.

Consider sharing with your accountability partner or another person. Describe your experience in a way that they can really feel. You might even want to make a short video to let more people hear you talk about it.

Playing in Business

Do this same exercise for your business.

What are you already experiencing in your business that's part of your vision?

Notice what's happening now. And call in those parts that are coming into this present moment.

Allow more pieces to become real. Right now.

Write about them.

Share about them.

Allow yourself to be supported in having them now.

And know that you can do the same for others in your community.

3. From *Having* a Vision to *Living* Your Vision

How do you know when you're living your vision?

Many of us have had the experience of buying a new car and then suddenly seeing that car everywhere. It's like we can think it into being, right?

What about your highest vision? Have you brought that into your life as well?

I've accomplished many things in my life. This is how I used to do it:

1. I had a goal.
2. I took the steps to get there.
3. I got there.
4. I set another goal. (Return to Step 1 and repeat.)

Every time I reached a goal, I'd move straight on to the next one. I wouldn't even pause to celebrate what I'd accomplished, as I was so focused on getting to the next goal.

Has this happened to you? Is this how you made your dreams come true?

In addition to more ordinary goals, I've even had visions come true—some faster than expected. When I was in school getting my teaching credential, I visualized my ideal job. My first job met every detail of that visualization. Then I realized I wasn't dreaming a big enough dream. It was just a plan.

That's the difference between choosing our vision and having our highest vision divinely shown to us. When we're given our highest vision from Spirit, it's usually a bit scary and we may not know how to manifest it. Many of us question whether it's even the right one for us. We resist. "Who, me?! I can't do that!" Have you felt that in response to your highest vision?

In this process of visiting your highest vision and drawing from that vision the answers to our questions, we're reminded that this is our *highest* vision. And we can dedicate ourselves to this process.

With our experiences of bringing things into our life, we know we can do this too. We know that Source gives us what's right for us. And Spirit provides for us what we need in order to have that vision become our reality. We know that this is our work in the world. But what if this "work" feels more like play when we're in alignment?

I've discovered that sometimes a vision isn't exactly how it looks in real life. But taking steps in that direction brings us to our desired experience here on earth.

Living your vision may be a feeling rather than an accomplishment. It may look different from how you initially envisioned it, but the *feeling* you got from your vision is what manifests in your life.

Keep tapping into your highest vision. If it's changing, allow it. Remember to look at your life now and see where you're already living your vision. Celebrate those areas. Invite friends over for a party and let them celebrate you! This is the part many of us forget to do. Celebrate!

And then rest in the knowing that you're following guidance on a regular basis. Keep following your dreams and keep using your voice to support you. And keep sharing about your experience in your journal and with people who can understand what you're doing.

And after you're well rested and you've celebrated your accomplishments, be curious about your next step.

4. Stay in Touch with Your Vision

Have you had a dream that you gave up on? Why is that? Is it that you lost interest? Or decided you just couldn't do it?

I had a vision that was so clear, but I couldn't complete it. I had the vision of a barn converted into a music school. I saw the big space for concerts and rehearsals of larger groups. I saw smaller classrooms for private and small-group instruction in all the different instruments and voices.

I collected images of barns from magazines to help me visualize my Music Farm. I even had a graphic designer create ads and business cards for me with the barn image I loved.

At the time, I was teaching private, small-group, and larger-group classes. I spoke with other music teachers who loved this vision and wanted to be a part of it. I was preparing to speak with a few key people in the community about being on my board of directors to help me bring the vision into reality.

Although I was on the path of doing so, I didn't have the divinely guided support I needed. As it turned out, I was diagnosed with breast cancer, which involved surgeries, radiation, and chemo. I had a few people helping me with my classes to keep the momentum going, but when I emerged from all of the treatments, I realized I couldn't keep going. I couldn't see my way to financially supporting this vision. I didn't have the energy to push it forward.

This speaks to the fact that it isn't only having support around you but having divinely guided support—a group of people and a special guide who can hold that divine vision for you when you're doubting yourself. People who know the truth about your vision and the power of bringing that into reality. And the vision itself has to be embedded in divine practices and big enough that it pulls you toward it.

It's never about pushing. If you're pushing your vision uphill, it's not your highest vision. Your highest vision will *pull* you toward it.

Let's Play!

I invite you to go back into that meditation from before (phoebefazio.com/book-extras) and revisit it if you're feeling like you need to push yourself in order to bring it into reality.

The bigger your vision, the more self-care you'll need.

Rather than pushing harder, I encourage you to:

- Take a salt bath.
- Go on a vacation.
- Do something fun to let go of the steering wheel for a while.
- Let the boat right itself and come back in line with the current of Divine Love.

- Spend more time in the dreaming, visioning state of mind.
- Play.
- Goof off.
- Rest deeply.

Source wants us to live our vision. They don't want us to exhaust ourselves in the process.

Keep in touch with your vision. Remember why you're doing the work you're doing. Remember why you're here on earth at this time. Remember that you are Love.

Journal Play

After you've gone back to your vision in meditation, spend some time writing down details from your vision.

- How do you feel in your vision?
- Can you feel yourself really living it?
- Spend as much time as possible feeling that.
- Write about it.
- What's something you could bring into your life that will feel like that?
- Ask for guidance and write affirmative prayers.

I encourage you to do this on a daily basis. Even multiple times a day. Write down what your day is like when your vision is real. Write that in present tense as if it's happening now.

Leave yourself love notes of encouragement, feeling grateful to your future self for inviting this into your life.

Sound Play

I invite you to continue your Voice Expression practice. While you're doing that, imagine you're living your vision.

- What will it look like when you're living your vision?
- Where will you practice your Voice Expression practice?
- How will that feel?
- What do you see around you?
- Who's there with you?

If you've been doing the seven-chakra Voice Expression practice, consider the twelve-chakra version. It may raise you to a higher vibrational space where you can attract your vision with more ease. Either one will assist you.

Share in your journal or with others:

- Do you struggle to do it every day?
- Do you do it every day and still struggle with your vision?

I know that you absolutely deserve to have your vision become your reality.

Playing in Business

Do all of the above for your business as well.

- What do you see in your vision that you aren't seeing in your life now?
- How can you stay in touch with the business you see for yourself?
- Who do you have to become to have that?
- What kind of support can you call upon to help you to bring it in?

VIII. Above and Beyond

1. The Four Clairs: Enhanced Psychic Abilities

Are you looking to open to your psychic abilities with more consistency and ease?

Are you wanting to strengthen and feel more connected to your clairs (clairvoyance, claircognizance, clairaudience, and clairsentience)?

Do you feel like you channel or you could channel, but you want to feel better about doing it?

When I began my journey with toning, I was also beginning my journey on the spiritual path. I had no idea where this was leading. I didn't think I had any psychic abilities, and I definitely wasn't thinking about channeling. I was a public school music teacher with no spiritual practices or beliefs. I didn't even know if I believed in God.

I only started working with an energy healer because she was a therapist. I was so down and depressed that I was willing to try anything, so when she offered something other than the usual talk therapy, I said, "Sure, why not?"

This energy work—along with activities such as spiritual-mind prayer work, a coaching program, meditation, yoga, Tai Chi, and Qigong— not only opened my voice but also opened me up to my gifts and abilities that many see as psychic. I began to notice my clairsentience (sensing energy or emotions through feeling) and my claircognizance (intuitive knowing that arises without logical explanation).

Also, my continued work with my own voice—through the Voice Expression practice and my Sound Washing—led me to understand that I was channeling sacred sounds. I came to understand that these sounds are encoded with messages. I learned that some of the sounds are forms of light language, which I could translate by speaking about what I was feeling in my body.

I discovered my clairvoyance along the way, as I was shown in a visual form the name of the "weird sounds" I was making. I saw "Sound Washing" across my field of vision one morning after doing my Voice Expression practice and meditating.

I notice that, for me, the visuals come when something is very important. I always take note when something is shown to me in that way.

Clairaudience comes while I'm making the sounds with my voice during sessions. I hear something in the sounds that guides me to the next sound and the next and the next. I don't hear words, but there's something in the vibration of the sounds that comes alive, and I follow it. I trust that what I'm hearing will guide me.

Even in everyday life, I notice sounds and can tune in to the deeper message in them or feel their nature. Sometimes it's soothing; sometimes it's agitating. And that's a message as well.

Let's Play!

Journal Play

I invite you to reflect on these questions and write down what comes to you in your journal.

- Do you know about your clairs?
- Which ones do you have? Clairvoyance? Clairaudience? Claircognizance? Clairsentience?
- Is one more dominant than others?
- Have you developed all of them?
- How do you use them in your life?
- If this is new to you, what do you imagine you would be able to sense through clairs?
- Consider what you find easier in life—seeing, hearing, knowing, or feeling—and write about your strengths in these areas.
- Write about what you'd like to add.
- Why do you want to get good at other clairs?
- How would that change your life?

Sound Play

Let's begin as we often do, with your Voice Expression practice.

While you're doing your practice, pay attention to how you feel around the Soul Star chakra.

You can complete your practice and then go a little deeper: consider playing with the sound "ih" of the Soul Star chakra.

Take the pitch up gently, allowing your voice to play like a dolphin jumping out of and diving back into the waves. Have fun.

As you play, tune in to the sensations in your body.

- What do you feel?
- What do you hear?
- What do you see?
- What do you come to understand?

Spend as much time as you'd like playing with your Soul Star in this way and tuning in to how it feels for you. Then spend some time writing in your journal or sharing with your accountability partner or others about what you noticed.

There are many other ways we can play, but start here and see where it takes you.

Playing in Business

Reflect on these questions about how the clairs relate to your business:

- Do you use the clairs in your healing work with your clients?
- Are there some that are more prevalent?
- Have you wanted to develop the others?
- Why do you want that?
- If you did develop your clairs, what would change in your work? How would that help your clients more? Would it help you reach more people?

- Sometimes, as healers, we want to learn new skills and develop our abilities. That's admirable. But what if instead of focusing on improving ourselves and our skills, we turn our focus to how we can help more people?
- How can you use the gifts you already have to expand your reach?
- How would it feel to reach more people with your gifts?
- What would change in your life?
- Would you feel more fulfilled?
- Would you earn more money?
- Would you feel more free?
- Does it scare you to help more people?
- Are you concerned about overworking and burning out? Maybe you've been there.

Share vulnerably about what comes up around this for you.

When you share honestly, you open the door for others to do the same. We can feel all the messy emotions and help one another.

2. How Voice Expression Practice Opens the Channel

Have you ever wondered how you could become a channel, to speak what's being downloaded to you?

Are you already a channeler and want to find a way to open to that channel more consistently or more easily?

Do you channel through writing or other avenues and want to be able to speak the messages directly?

When I started doing the Voice Expression practice daily, I discovered that I was able to speak and write messages more clearly and easily.

By helping others with my Sound Washings and receiving feedback, I discovered I was channeling. I could hear that the sounds were like Tibetan monks, Mongolian nuns, angels, animals, astral beings, and more, but I hadn't tuned in to the messages. I trusted that the sounds were doing their work for whoever heard them. I didn't feel like I needed to know exactly what was being said. Yet when asked about the meaning or the message, I was able to tune in and answer with words that gave meaning to these sound messages. I also knew they were encoded with light and energy that transcended words.

I found that I had part of the translation and the client had the other part. Together we were able to decipher some of the messages. However, I came to understand that we didn't need to understand with our minds. Our bodies can get it on another level.

That's how it happened for me.

Meanwhile, behind the scenes, I was doing my Voice Expression practice every day. As I did, I was aligning my energy. I was clearing out old stuck energies and bringing in fresh new energy. I was balancing my energy, my mind, and my body.

This Voice Expression practice is multifaceted. It works on many levels at the same time. So the more I did it, the more awakened I became. My gifts became more alive in me, and I became more aware of them.

As I've found, this is a daily practice. The results don't come overnight. Small steps over time create results.

When I met with other channelers as part of my Global Channeling Summit, I felt validated and reassured that channeling was a gift. I also learned that there are various types of channeling. Not everyone channels by speaking. Some hear the messages and then translate them. Others speak while they're connected (sometimes with a voice that sounds different from their normal speaking voice). Some write the messages as they come through, while others write as a translation of what they receive, which may be in the form of images or other transmissions.

The channeling I do comes through sound and light language. I speak afterward, explaining the sounds through messages that I feel are also channeled. I also channel business information for healers. When they start telling me their vision, I get downloads for their path to prosperity.

I feel that my channeling is connected with my Reiki practice. I'm a Reiki Master, which means I have three levels of attunements. This gives me the ability to channel Universal Love and Light through my being and share it with a person or out to the world. I receive the benefits as well.

I believe that working with this channel of Universal Love and Light energy is what allows me to channel sounds and words. I don't know if that's a requirement, but if you're trying these exercises and feeling like it's not quite getting you where you want to go, then maybe look into being attuned in Reiki or other energy modalities. Reiki is accessible and available to all who seek it.

If you're being called to be a Reiki healer, reach out to me (see contact information at the end of this book). I can get you started on your path if you feel it resonates.

Let's Play!

Are you interested in being a channel?

How are you wanting to channel?

How do you already channel?

What do you feel your message is?

Do you have a sense of who you could help with your channeling?

As we explore the possibilities of channeling, begin by doing your regular practice—and have your journal handy.

Journal Play

In the silence following your Voice Expression practice, write freely. Write down anything that occurs to you. You might even consider using your nondominant hand to see if anything comes that way.

If the words are flowing, allow them.

If nothing happens, then here are some prompts you can use:

- What does it mean to you to channel?
- Why do you want to channel?
- If you already channel, what are you wanting to shift?
- Can you identify how that would feel?

Sound Play

We can play with the Galactic Gateway a little bit here.

Pause your writing for a moment.

Ask the question you have about channeling as you make the sound "rr."

Breathe in, make the sound on the exhale, breathe in, "rr," breathe in, "rr. . . ."

Stay with it until you feel complete or you have an answer.

Whether or not you know what to write, put your pen to the paper and begin writing. Use either hand—or try them both. See what comes.

If writing is not really your preferred approach or you're wanting to channel with your voice, I encourage you to use your phone (or other recording device). Open your voice-recording app and just start talking. If you don't have a voice recorder, you can use your camera and make a video.

You might never watch that video. Just use it to test out your theory about what your channeling style is. Maybe what comes out are "weird sounds," like what happened to me. Maybe you notice that those sounds are like some of the chakra sounds in the Voice Expression practice. Allow it to be what it is.

The first time my "weird sounds" became words was when I was saying "I am" so slowly I didn't recognize what I was saying. So let the sounds come. Whether they're words or not, just stay with the practice.

Don't work too hard at it. Leave it if you feel any tension or frustration. And come back again another time. Another day.

Share with your accountability partner or your community. See where you can find some encouragement. You aren't doing anything wrong. Everything is right.

Playing in Business

Is channeling a part of your healing business?

How do you use it?

Do you want to add channeling to your gifts?

Why do you want that?

What will that mean for you and for your clients?

Doing your Voice Expression practice is activating and aligning all your chakras. And opening the Galactic Gateway is opening the channel. So, even if you aren't already channeling, you're primed and ready.

Write about how your business would improve if you were channeling in the way you desire.

What's in the way of you having that?

Regardless of whether you channel, the Galactic Gateway opens to the infinite. So when you tap into that chakra, you can be, do, or have whatever you desire. I invite you to play with it and bring that energy into the areas of your business that you want to improve so you can live your vision.

Sometimes we also need to talk with a human about these things. I understand. I'm human too. And I love to listen. Perhaps there's someone in your life who you trust to listen.

3. Qigong with Voice Expression Practice

Are you a kinesthetic learner?

Do you learn best by doing? By moving your body?

Is it easier to really understand something when you can feel it in your body?

I'm a kinesthetic learner. In my teaching-credential training, we learned all about the different learning styles: visual, auditory, tactile, musical, etc. And I discovered that I learn best when I can embody what's being taught.

When I was growing up, however, schools didn't cater to different learning styles. You just did what you were told. There was a lot of listening and some visual aids. So I adapted. And then I realized that I was an active kid—I was on the swim team, and also loved gymnastics, tennis, riding bikes, roller skating, playing outside.

Later on, I learned to dance (ballet) and in college studied modern dance, which is a freer form of ballet where we learned how our bodies moved. And I was still swimming, riding my bike, running, and moving my body every chance I got.

Studying music was somewhat kinesthetic. I realized that when I memorized piano pieces, it was muscle memory more than mental memory.

As I came to the Voice Expression practice, I felt the sounds and vibrations in my body. Do you feel it in your body as well? That felt kinesthetic enough for me.

In recent years, I've studied Tai Chi and Qigong. What many people understand as a form of exercise (that's slow and gentle enough for aging bodies), I learned was a form of energy work—moving the energy with the body.

I could feel the energy.

I'd already studied Reiki and understood how I could use energy for healing but hadn't really felt it the way I did when I did Tai Chi and Qigong.

I studied Tai Chi and Qigong from various teachers and was very consistent with my studies during the time that I lived with my mom at the end of her life. I was in the caregiver role and needed to have a place to go to recharge. This practice was so helpful for that.

Because I did it regularly, it became a part of me. Something I did daily for my body.

One day recently on my walk, I started to combine my Voice Expression practice with the repetitive movements of Qigong.

Over the years, I've noticed that although my Voice Expression practice mostly stays consistent, it's a living practice that evolves over time. I get ideas and insights to try here and there. Below, I share one of those insights—something you might consider if you want to feel the power of the sounds and the energy flow in your body a bit more kinesthetically, whether or not you've studied Tai Chi or Qigong.

Let's Play!

Journal Play

Before or after you test out these movements, take a few moments to write.

- How do you see yourself learning with your body?
- Do you find that when you move your body, you "get it" more completely?
- Have you always known that you were a kinesthetic learner? How did you know?
- What other styles of learning are you aware of in yourself?

Sound Play

Let's play with movement and sound together.

If you're not familiar with Qigong, the basic idea is that you're moving energy with your hands. With relaxed hands and relaxed arms, you can "gather" energy and draw it into your body. You can also use these same movements to move energy out. Here we're gathering.

For each chakra, we'll gather energy either from the earth (below) or the sky (above).

We'll go through the twelve-chakra system here, but you can do just the seven if that's the Voice Expression practice version you're using.

Before beginning, practice gathering energy from above. Standing, reach your arms out to the side and a little bit in front, palms up. Then raise your arms up overhead, gather, and draw your hands toward each other and float them down in front of your body. Relax your arms and hands at the bottom, then repeat three or more times.

When you're ready, try this sequence while you use your voice to tone the chakra:

1. Bend at the waist, reaching the arms down, gathering up Earth energy that flows up between the legs, and standing straight as you gather the energy and make the sound with your voice. Repeat as many times as you'd like for each of the first three sounds:
   - *Earth Star* – Mm-vv-zz
   - *Root* – Uh
   - *Sacral* – Oo
2. Reach out in front and gather energy toward each of these chakras as you make these sounds with your voice:
   - *Solar Plexus* – Oh
   - *Heart* – Aw
   - *High Heart* – Ah
   - *Throat* – Ay
3. Reaching overhead in a relaxed manner (shoulders relaxed down), gather from above as you make these sounds with your voice. Allow the energy to flow in from

the Divine, down into all areas of your body after each focused chakra:

- *Brow* – Eye
- *Cranial* – Ng
- *Crown* – Ee
- *Soul Star* – Ih
- *Galactic Gateway* – Rr

If you've done Qigong (or other energy practices) before, you may intuit more ways to move energy as you make the sounds.

Make this practice your own if it feels good.

I invite you to share in written or spoken words with your accountability partner or a community what you're feeling and noticing from this practice. Will you do it more? Why or why not?

Playing in Business

Do you ever get up from your desk and move around when you need a break from what you're doing?

Do you have a movement practice that you do daily? Or a few times a week?

If movement is what gets you going, then maybe this Qigong addition to your Voice Expression practice will assist you as well.

Sometimes it might even be helpful to focus on moving the energy around that one part of your business that's feeling a bit sticky or where you want to have more movement. For instance, if you're feeling the need or desire for more income, maybe move the energy around your sacral chakra and tone the "oo" sound.

Or if you're trying to make a video and are feeling stuck about what to say, try moving the energy around your solar plexus and toning the "oh" sound.

Test it out for other areas in your business. You can use the "7 Proven Steps" checklist (Appendix C) and the full-color chart of the chakra tones (available at phoebefazio.com/book-extras) to remind you of which areas align with which chakras.

Then be sure to write about it in your journal. And share with your accountability partner and community.

- What did you notice?
- What shifted when you tried these movement practices?
- What did you try?
- What worked for you?
- Is that where it ends?
- How about your next steps? Where will you go from here?

CONCLUSION

Your Journey

You've been on quite a journey with your voice and your vision. Here's what we've covered:

We started with the tones for the seven chakras and the different emotions and life experiences that could be getting in your way of living the life of your dreams.

Then we used those seven chakra tones and your new awareness to take you into discovering your highest vision.

We went deeper into the Voice Expression practice with the twelve-chakra system and more awareness, followed by a deeper understanding of our highest vision, our next steps, and how we can bring our vision into our current reality.

We wrapped up with going beyond our understanding of our voice and our highest vision to see what is possible.

Now What?

Where can you go from here?

If you're clear on your vision and are bringing it into reality with your regular Voice Expression practice, then you're already taking your next steps.

If you feel like you need more, you could go back through the sections you struggled with and revisit the "Journal Play" and "Sound Play" sections.

Keep doing your Voice Expression practice on a daily basis and you'll find your flow with it.

If you still have more questions and would like to reach out, you can find me here: phoebe@phoebefazio.com.

If you'd like a little more support with this work—with your voice, your vision, or your business—reach out and let's chat a bit to see how I can be of service. Or if you'd like to share about your experience with this book, I'd love to hear from you. I appreciate learning about other people's perspectives, and it can also be very helpful for you to share with someone in order to bring your vision to life—another way of using your voice!

It's been my pleasure to guide you through these profound practices. I send you great blessings of love and light as you bring your voice and vision more powerfully into the world.

APPENDICES

Appendix A: Toning the 7 Chakras

Tone each chakra in turn, beginning at the root and moving upward to the crown.

- Root (red): "uh"
- Sacral (orange): "oo"
- Solar Plexus (yellow): "oh"
- Heart (green): "aw"
- Throat (blue): "ay"
- Brow (indigo): "eye"
- Crown (violet): "ee"

To see a full-color version of this chart, please visit my book extras page: phoebefazio.com/book-extras.

Appendix B: The 12-Chakra Tones

The full twelve-chakra system, in order, from the Earth Star up to the Galactic Gateway.

- Earth Star (black): "mm-vv-zz"
- Root (red): "uh"
- Sacral (orange): "oo"
- Solar Plexus (yellow): "oh"
- Heart (green): "aw"
- High Heart (turquoise): "ah"
- Throat (light blue): "ay"
- Brow (dark blue): "eye"
- Cranial (violet): "ng"
- Crown (purple): "ee"
- Soul Star (magenta): "ih"
- Galactic Gateway (white): "rr"

To see a full-color version of this chart, please visit my book extras page: phoebefazio.com/book-extras.

Appendix C: 7 Proven Steps to Grow Your Healing Business Online

For healers and channelers ready to channel their business, this process will help you:

- Attract Your Ideal Clients
- Turn Your Passion into Profit
- Make a Living with Your Gifts

7 Proven Steps

1. **Platform – Online Presence:** Establish the foundation for your online healing business (social media, website, etc.) so that you can show up for your clients.
2. **People – Who You Help:** Define your ideal, divine clients so that you know who you are attracting.
3. **Shine – Spiritual Marketing:** Show up (video, text, photos, audio) so that your clients can find you.
4. **Service – Your Marketable Program:** Design your transformational program so that you can deliver your gifts to your divine clients.
5. **Speak – Make Offers:** Share about your program with clarity so that you can invite clients and get paid.
6. **Vision – Your Highest Vision:** Tap into your divine guidance daily so that you move forward powerfully.

7. **Practice – Spiritual and Practical:** Practice daily spiritual habits and your business skills so that you can show up fully resourced.

Support – You Can Do This

Surround yourself with supportive people who can guide you toward your vision so that you don't get lost in self-doubt.

To see a full-color version of this guide, please visit my book extras page: phoebefazio.com/book-extras.

Appendix D: Resources

The books, recordings, and programs referred to throughout these pages, for readers who'd like to explore them further.

- Campbell, Don. *Healing Yourself with Your Own Voice* (audio program).
- Goldman, Jonathan. *Vocal Toning the Chakras* (audio program).
- Keyes, Laurel Elizabeth. *Toning: The Creative Power of the Voice* (book).
- Lamond, Bill. *Fulfillment-Based Thinking* (coaching program).
- Progoff, Ira. *At a Journal Workshop* (book featuring the Intensive Journal method).
- Robinson, Ray, and Allen Winold. *The Choral Experience: Literature, Materials, and Methods* (book).

About the Author

Phoebe Fazio is an award-winning speaker, best-selling author, sound healer, and Reiki Master whose work bridges music, energy medicine, and conscious self-expression.

With over twenty-five years of experience teaching music in public schools, Phoebe has spent her life immersed in sound—listening to it, shaping it, teaching it, and ultimately discovering its profound power to heal, regulate the nervous system, and awaken deeper states of awareness. Her deep understanding of voice, breath, vibration, and resonance forms the foundation of her work today.

Through her signature modality, Sound Washing, Phoebe offers immersive sound-healing experiences, concerts, workshops, and speaking engagements both in person and online. Her work invites people into deep presence, relaxation, emotional release, and inner clarity—creating spaces where transformation happens gently and naturally.

As a Reiki Master and intuitive guide, Phoebe also supports those who feel called to work with energy medicine, offering attunements and mentorship grounded in integrity, compassion, and deep listening. Her approach is experiential rather than prescriptive, honoring each individual's unique rhythm, sensitivity, and inner wisdom.

Phoebe's journey has been shaped not only by decades of teaching and training, but also by her own profound healing path. Through personal challenges, including a life-altering health journey, she was guided back to the voice—not as performance, but as prayer, medicine, and truth. This lived experience brings depth, humility, and heartfelt presence into all of her work.

In *Voice & Vision: Use Your Voice to Bring Your Vision to Life*, Phoebe weaves together sound, breath, awareness, and gentle inquiry to guide readers back into alignment with their authentic voice and deepest knowing. Her writing reflects the same qualities that define her teaching: clarity, warmth, spaciousness, and deep respect for each person's inner journey.

Phoebe believes that when we reconnect with our voice, we remember who we are—and from that remembering, life begins to move with greater ease, purpose, and flow.

Contact Information

Feel free to reach out to connect or ask questions.

Email: phoebe@phoebefazio.com

Website: https://phoebefazio.com

Book Extras: phoebefazio.com/book-extras

Scan for Book Extras

Made in United States
Troutdale, OR
08/19/2026

53122161R00166